All Tanked

the Canadians in Heaaiey during World War II

When Canadian troops arrived in Great Britain during the Second World War, they were given quarters in old, cold, damp barracks buildings in the military town of Aldershot. For these young men thousands of miles from home, and in many cases away from their families for the first time, it was a depressing experience.

Imagine their joy then, when they found their next station in England was not another military camp, but a charming rural village with pubs, girls, dances – and a welcome for them from the local population.

All Tanked Up is the story of their benign 'invasion' of a Hampshire village over a period of four years, told from the point of view of both Villagers and Canadians.

For those to whom 'Peace in our Time' came too late.

Cover: Montage of Headley scenes by Hester Whittle

All Tanked Up

the Canadians in Headley during World War II

*compiled from the memories
of Villagers and Veterans*

by John Owen Smith

All Tanked Up
First published May 1994
This edition published 2008

Typeset and published by John Owen Smith
19 Kay Crescent, Headley Down, Hampshire GU35 8AH

Tel: 01428 712892
wordsmith@johnowensmith.co.uk
www.johnowensmith.co.uk

© John Owen Smith 1994 & 2008

ISBN 978-1873855-54-6

[Replacing ISBN 1-873855-00-1]

Printed and bound by CPI Antony Rowe, Eastbourne

Contents

Illustrations & Maps

Source of Illustrations acknowledged where known
All recent photographs by the author

Author's Note

During a summer visit in 1993 to a particularly peaceful location in our area with members of The Headley Society, talk turned to recollections of other less restful times. Thoughts of the 50th anniversary of D-Day, coming up in June 1994, brought back memories to those who were in the village then, of tanks negotiating narrow lanes and Canadian troops packing the pubs. Surely someone should write a history of it all, while people were still around to tell the tale, they said. And so the project started.

We had a certain amount of information to hand locally: lists of regiments which had stayed in the village, back copies of local newspapers, parish magazines and, of course, the memories of those who were here. But to get the Canadian point of view, I decided to advertise in their Veterans' magazines, both in Britain and in Canada, for anyone who remembered Headley. I'd thought this might draw a blank, but I needn't have worried – every week seemed to bring new letters and fascinating stories from across the Atlantic and, conveniently, addresses of several Canadian ex-servicemen now living in England.

In particular I wanted to discover facts about Erie Camp, the military detention centre situated where Heatherlands now stands, and was delighted when one of the letters from Canada turned out to be from an ex-inmate, who was able to give me an informative and amusing, if in parts unpublishable, view of life behind the wire.

Visiting museums, reading regimental histories and talking to those who had served in armoured divisions gave me background material to add to the personal stories of men who had passed through the village on their way to Normandy or Italy, and one lucky find in a local house-clearance sale brought me notes from a wartime course on 'how to service armoured vehicles'.

Stories of wartime are bitter-sweet affairs – a mixture of pride and poignancy extends through both personal and public events. The story I'm telling belongs not to me, but to the people of Headley and Canada who entrusted me with their memories, and I thank them for so willingly volunteering their information. I have tried where possible to let their voices speak, and keep my own comments and additions to a minimum – after all, I wasn't there at the time and they were. I sincerely hope both they and many others will enjoy reading the book.

John Owen Smith
Headley, 1994

Additional Note to the 2008 Edition

Since *All Tanked Up* was first published, in May 1994, I have had the happy experience of meeting and corresponding further with a number of people, some original contributors and some new, many of whose extra stories and pictures I have been able to add to this edition.

In particular I would like to thank Gord Crossley, Fort Garry Archivist, who visited Headley in 2000 while he was doing research for the regiment and again in 2007 and has been of great help to me in matters related to Canadian military history. He was kind enough to present the village with a Fort Garry Horse regimental shield, which is now a prized possession.

I was also touched to receive, out of the blue, some Fort Garry Horse lapel badges from Erle Kitching via a mutual friend who met him during Normandy commemorations in 2002. My thanks to him.

My thanks, indeed, to all those veterans who have looked me up when revisiting Headley since the book was first published – I have enjoyed swapping yarns and sharing a beer with you!

Sadly, I am all too aware that some of my original contributors are now no longer with us. As I explained in my original note, this project was originally proposed to me as a way of keeping alive memories which might otherwise soon disappear, and I hope I have in some measure achieved that.

However, do please do keep the information coming in – there are still plenty of blank spots to fill in the history. Those with internet access may like to look up **www.johnowensmith.co.uk/canadians.htm** to see any new material we may gather, and also use this as a means of getting in touch with me electronically.

John Owen Smith
Headley, 2008

General Map of the Area

Including Bentley to Bordon branch railway line and Longmoor Military Railway, both now closed.

Note that Frensham Great and Little Ponds were drained during the war, to prevent enemy aircraft using them as navigational aids.

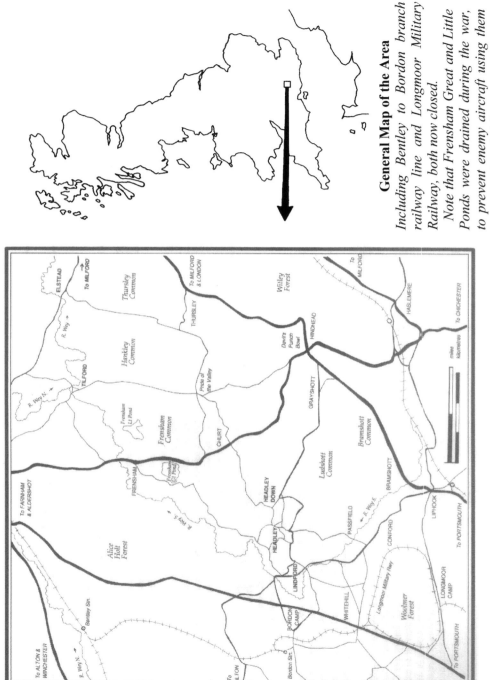

All Tanked Up …

Introduction

The village of Headley sits just across the River Wey from Bordon Camp. This was constructed at the turn of the century on land first purchased by the army in 1863 for use as a training area and, until the end of the 1920s, formed an integral part of Headley parish. Through the years, therefore, the village has become familiar with the presence of the military close at hand. Older residents tell of hearing the bugle calls from the Camp, and today we can hear quite distinctly the firing coming from the Woolmer ranges.

During the First World War, villagers saw troops, led by their military bands, marching through from Bordon to Ludshott Common in order to practice digging trenches. They remember a meat depot and bakery being established on the Village Green, bread being baked in open ovens for the soldiers of several local camps, and the Institute adjoining the back of the Congregational Chapel (both since demolished) being used to give soldiers a cup of tea on Sunday afternoons.

Sadly, all too few years were to pass before the village and common were again used for similar purposes.

The Village Prepares

Britain declared war on Germany on 3rd September 1939 and, as Mrs Katie Warner puts it, "immediately there were plans made to billet soldiers everywhere in the village." She lived in the School House at the time, and recalls that initially tents were erected on the Village Green, and a field cookhouse "like a huge saucepan for producing stew" arrived to provide hot food for the soldiers there. Winter was soon upon them – that first year there was a lot of snow – and when eventually it began to thaw, the soldiers were "ploughing around ankle deep in mud."

In fact that winter was the coldest on record since 1894, although this could not be publicised at the time, as the weather was a military secret during the war.

A number of houses, such as *Belmont* in the High Street, were already owned by the Army, but others in the area were quickly requisitioned. Herbert Price with 'D' Company of the 1/6th South Staffordshire Regiment was billeted in *The Mount*, through the archway at the top of Barley Mow Hill, from October 1939 until March 1940. In letters written to Pauline Grove, who lives there now, he says: "That winter was very cold, and I remember the trees were all turned more or less into glass. The track from *The Mount* was very rough, and we used to 'Get fell in' and march, or rather slide, down the track to the Green where the marquees were set up to serve as dining quarters. Very primitive, but looking back it was fun. Frozen tea, spuds, veg, you name it and we had it."

The tents remained on the Green for "maybe the best part of a year," according to Katie Warner, while other more permanent accommodation was found or built. Nissen Huts were constructed in the Rectory Field, on the Village Green and elsewhere in the village, and eventually a proper brick canteen was built on the Green during 1941. At the top of Rectory Field there were also two dining halls, which were of brick, "but they never had roofs put on – they had huge canvas marquees put over them instead." *Apparently there was a similar pair erected on Crestafield along with a NAAFI according to David Whittle, one used as a dining room and the other, he thinks, as a QM stores.*

"We didn't have a lot of pay in 1939," says Herbert Price, "but what we had we were happy to spend on Friday and Saturday evenings in the *Wheatsheaf*. Mostly though, during the week, we used to frequent the tea room in the village for a cuppa, and sometimes a cake. My memories of Headley are very pleasant. I can see that room now, round tables, flowers in the middle, home from home."

I have been told there was a tea room at the bottom of Barley Mow Hill. Also, the words 'Headley Restaurant' were, according to Sue Allden, painted on the side wall of Radford's Shop, now Long Cross House, but removed as a security measure when the war began.

"We were inspected by HM the King and Queen at Bordon prior to going to France with the BEF. I wonder how many recall that, in 1940? It was a fair march from Headley."

There were other British regiments stationed in the village at this early stage in the war. Betty Roquette's cousin by marriage, Lord George Scott who was Colonel in charge of Hussars, was billeted in *Beech Hill House*. Ironically her brother, Jim Richards, was also here later as part of the Canadian Provost Company guarding Erie Camp just up the hill, but the two men never knew each other.

Betty Parker remembers the South Staffordshires, Jim Clark the 9th Lancers and the 10th Hussars, and Joyce Stevens also recalls the latter, mostly conscripts she thinks, who were here for some time. Arthur Dean remembers they were parked in Headley, "for a long time in the early part of the war – mainly up from the *Wheatsheaf* alongside the road – and they had the old Crusader tanks."

But eventually the British troops left, and Headley's special relationship with the Canadians was to begin.

Old Renault tank bought from the USA for training in Canada..
Pete Friesen of the Fort Garrys in camp Borden, Ontario
before their regiment shipped to Britain

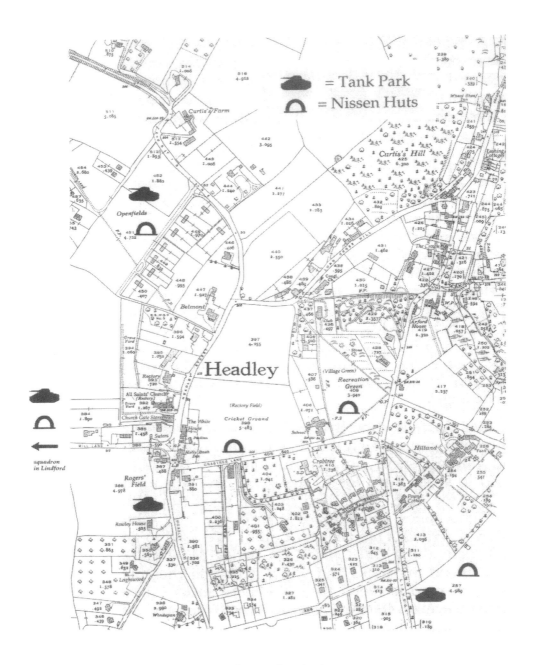

Headley and Arford
Showing position of Tank Parks and Nissen Huts 1942–44
(base map dated 1937, with some later additions)

See pages 24–25 for map of Headley Down

The Canadians Arrive

Canada declared war on 10th September 1939, and the first 'flight' of Canadian troops for Britain sailed in a convoy from Halifax, Nova Scotia to arrive safely in the Clyde on 17th December of that year. The 7,400 servicemen on board included men from Infantry regiments, the Army Service Corps and the 'Mounties'. The latter formed the No 1 Provost Company, some of whom were to serve, like Jim Richards, in Headley as 'provos', supervising the Canadian military detention centre. Many further 'flights' followed over the next 4 to 5 years, bringing a large variety of Canadian regiments to these shores. During the whole of this time only one ship carrying Canadian troops was torpedoed.

It seems that no Canadian troops were stationed in Headley itself until 1941, but several of their service units were located in Bordon from the early days of the war and, since Headley was regarded as a good place in which to 'get away', Canadian soldiers soon became a familiar sight in the village. Not all of the resulting encounters were as cordial as might be hoped. Tom Grisdale, who ran a poultry farm in Liphook Road at the time, recalls: "One night I looked out of the window and saw a light down the field. I took my gun and a torch, and found two French Canadians who'd just hunted this sack full of chickens. Fortunately they hadn't killed them, so I rammed the gun in their backs and they dropped the sack and put their hands up. They said if I let them go they wouldn't come again, so I did – otherwise I thought I'd probably have the whole regiment."

John Ellis (who later was to transport American armour to Utah Beach in LCTs) also remembers the Canadians' partiality for supplementing their rations with local fresh meat. He says: "Before 1943, we had a pig farm adjoining the stores and buildings at Headley Mill, including a breeding section. One night, someone got into the pigsties and took a whole litter of suckling pigs. In the morning, the sow was standing there alone, and we found a full bottle of beer, which had been used to stun the pigs, and a forage cap complete with the badge of the Canadian Provost Corps!" On another occasion, one moonlit night near Christmas time, his sister saw some Canadian soldiers strip off and plunge into the ice cold water of the mill pond to try and catch the geese there – but this time they failed.[†]

[†] See aerial view of Headley Mill, p.44

Royal Canadian Engineers Constructing Erie Camp, August 1941

"The Sewer Rats"
The RCE sewer construction gang at the 'Headley Army Detention Camp'

RCE shoulder patch

Phil Herring surveying

The Canadians also had their own reservations about some of our British ways. One ex-soldier recalled that British instructors tried to teach him, unsuccessfully, how to bowl a grenade. Another remembers the very elderly Brigadier who, "at the completion of our training at a battle school in Wales explained the purpose of the final exercise: 'You Canadian chaps will be the Swazi tribesmen in the hills and we British will dislodge you.' Churchill was saying Nazis while the Brigadier was saying Swazis, and Lord it was a confusing war for us at the muddy boots level."

A detachment of 6th Field Company Royal Canadian Engineers 3rd Division arrived in Headley on 16th July 1941, with instructions to build a military prison camp. Tom Grisdale recalls that it was built using timber brought all the way over from Canada. It was to be on "what seemed to be a piece of wasteland," according to Fergus Steele, who helped construct it. They lived in tents nearby and "completed the job about the middle of October." This 'wasteland' was part of the Land of Nod, owned by Major Whitaker, and some villagers still remember it as being "the prettiest spot in Headley – wonderful view from there – pure unspoilt common land, heath, pines and heather." It became Erie Camp, now Heatherlands Estate.

Whether by coincidence or design, the new Headley Down automatic telephone exchange opened at about the same time as Erie Camp was completed. It stood halfway down Glayshers Hill, just across the road from the camp, in a building dated 1939. We have records showing that the phone number given to the 'Canadian Detention Barracks' was Headley Down 2174.

The first stage of sewer construction passes the test.
The picture shows there are 6 outlets to a manhole –
one from each plumbing fixture in the building.

During September 1941, while the Detention Barracks were still being built, the Calgary Regiment moved into Headley having lived under canvas on Salisbury Plain for a couple of months since arriving in the country. It was one of three regiments in the 1st Canadian Army Tank Brigade, which was now being concentrated "in the Farnham area" to perform training "on the moors" with the 3rd Canadian Infantry Division.

The Calgarys arrived with old 'Waltzing Matilda' tanks, but these were soon replaced by new Churchills. Jim Clark remembers watching them waterproofing the Churchills on Openfields – "putting black bituminous stuff, round the doors on the side," and Arthur Dean, whose sister married Jim Hanczin of the Calgarys, recalls: "we used to go up to Rogers Field, by the *Holly Bush*, and see them putting waterproofing all round the turrets – they put thick tape over the joints and anything that opened or moved – then they got the exhausts right up in the air, so they could go through the water."

"We knew something was *on*", Jim Clark said – and suddenly they all left and never came back.

He links this in his mind with the raid on Dieppe, in which the Calgary Regiment was involved, but regimental records show that they left Headley in December 1941 to take up a role guarding the South Coast of England, eight months before the Dieppe operation occurred.

This mystery seems to have been solved by Steve Dyson who, in his book *Tank Twins*, tells us that the 107 Regt (King's Own) R.A.C. was stationed with Churchill tanks in Headley from early April 1944 until they left for Normandy on 23rd June. He says:— *Once established in our billets [in Headley] we soon got down to the urgent preparation of waterproofing the tanks... Extension ducts had to be fitted to the air inlet vents on either side of the hull, and long extension pipes to the exhaust system. Rivets and bolts cleaned and painted with waterproof paint. Inspection covers and, in fact, all areas where water could penetrate, were sealed with a rubber compound. Balloon fabric was glued around the ring of the turret, the gun mountings, and driver's visor, under which ran a continuous length of cordex which, when detonated from a switch in the driver's compartment, exploded and blew it all off so that the tank could immediately go into action if necessary.*

It would appear to have been the Churchills of this British regiment which Jim Clark and others saw being waterproofed in Headley, not those of the Calgary regiment after all – and Jim later agreed that this may well be so.

Fooling the Germans

A story from Dennis G Scott CM, President 50/14 Veterans' Association

The 14th Canadian Armoured Regiment (Calgary tanks) was training on Headley Down near Grayshott, England in October 1941. One Saturday afternoon when 'F' Troop 'C' Squadron was on duty, we received a visit from some HQ Brass, two British Officers and a BBC film crew. They wanted a Tank and crew for some action shots. Our Troop Officer was away so Cpl Herb Travis was ordered to mount a crew and prepare to take a tank onto the training area.

The catch came when German uniforms were produced and the crew was told to put them on. Cpl Travis refused and was put on orders. They turned to another NCO who complied.

The crew were told to take the tank out onto the training area and drive it over a prepared course which would end when they were enveloped in smoke bombs and thunder flashes. They were to evacuate the tank and emerge from the smoke with their hands above their heads. This done the visitors left and the tank crew returned to base.

On Monday morning, Cpl Travis was taken before the CO and was demoted to Tpr for refusing to carry out an order. A couple of nights later we were at a theatre in Haslemere watching the usual Pathé News when our 'C' Squadron crew were shown emerging from the smoke on Headley Down with their hands up over the caption "British 8th Army destroys Panzer in North Africa."

When Troop Officer Lt. Bryce Douglas returned to camp and discovered that one of his Cpls had been stripped he was incensed. He asked Travis why he had refused the order. Travis explained that his father had been killed by the Germans in World War One and there was no way that he would put a German uniform on. Douglas agreed and Travis had his stripes back.

Dennis Scott tells us: "We had arrived in England July 1st, 1941 and went directly to Salisbury Plains for July and August and, after going to Wales for gunnery practise, we arrived at Headley. From Headley we went to Seaford until April when we went to the Isle of White to train for the Dieppe Raid. We had landing practice at Gosport and returned to Seaford where we embarked for Dieppe. Dieppe was the end of the war for me as I was taken prisoner there."

Overleaf is a copy of a propaganda leaflet which was dropped over southern England by the Germans after the raid had failed.

Propaganda Leaflet dropped by Germans over southern England after the Dieppe raid

Many of the Churchill tanks in these pictures were delivered to the Calgary Regiment while it was stationed in Headley

A Popular Station

The largest body of troops to sail from Canada during the war embarked at Halifax in November 1941, and included the 5th Canadian Armoured Division. The convoy of 12 liners arrived on this side of the Atlantic on 22nd/23rd November. On landing in Britain, the regiments were first sent by rail to Aldershot, and Pete Friesen of the Fort Garry Horse remembers marching from Aldershot station through the town at midnight to full musical accompaniment from their trumpeters, of whom he was one, and being booed by the residents for waking them.

They stayed there in old, cold barracks which were not at all popular. As Pat Lewis of the Sherbrooke Fusiliers, who came along the same route a year later, said: "Nobody liked Aldershot – you got one bucket of coke and a few bits of wood and you had a grate, and that's all you had to heat a massive room – and there were 15 people in that room. As soon as you had a penny in your pocket you ran out of there as fast as you could go – sometimes you didn't know where you were going to – you just got on a bus and went somewhere, anywhere." Pete Friesen added that the piles of coke in Aldershot barracks used to be sprayed white so that the authorities could see if anyone had been stealing it overnight.

After a few weeks, the regiments were moved to other locations more suitable for tank training. One of these was Headley, and the official history of the Lord Strathcona's Horse recollects that "the march from Aldershot to Headley was one of the most pleasant ever made, through small lanes." It includes a photograph taken of the men marching along what could be Bacon Lane, although the location is untitled, and continues: "On arrival, the troops were delighted to find that the new billets were requisitioned civilian houses which, although not mansions, were vastly more pleasant than the damp, dark barracks of Aldershot." They were also to live in Squadron groups (of about 80 to 90 men) for the first time. "The final item which filled our cup to overflowing was the fact that a short 15 minute walk in any of three directions brought us to one of 3 delightful country pubs. One of these, *The Wheatsheaf*, was perhaps a little too handy, as the members of 'A' Squadron will remember."

This was April 1942, a time of many Canadian arrivals in the area. Men from other armoured regiments also marched or drove along the lanes from Aldershot during the month, including the Fort Garry Horse, who were to become the best known regiment in the village, as they and their mascot 'Whitey' were stationed here not once, but twice during the run up to D-Day. Their official record states that Headley "proved to be one of our most popular stations; we soon got to know the natives, who we found very agreeable – it was really our first meet up with the English folk." Each regiment had a compliment of 660 'all ranks', and at least two regiments at a time were stationed here, so accommodation for more than 1,300 men must have been required in and around the village.

There were normally three regiments attached to an armoured Division or Brigade, and these tended to move station together. In the case of the 5th Canadian Armoured Division, two regiments (Fort Garry Horse and Lord Strathcona's Horse) were placed in the Headley area, while the third (1st Hussars) was placed in the Elstead area. This continued to be the pattern for future postings here.

The 5th Division, which at this time included the British Columbia Dragoons who are also reported to have come here, stayed for about 4 months, until the beginning of August 1942, then left for Hove. Shortly afterwards, three regiments of the 4th Division arrived in the area: the Elgin Regiment, the South Alberta Regiment, and the British Columbia Regiment, who also stayed with us for about 4 months.

The first two of these were replaced in January 1943 by other regiments of the 4th Division, at a time when the Canadian Armoured Divisions were being re-organised. The Governor General's Foot Guards and the Canadian Grenadier Guards stayed for about a month before they moved on. Marcel Fortier of the Foot Guards notes: "The citizens received us with customary English reserve, but this atmosphere soon gave way to one of warm hospitality. Headley became one of the homes that was eventually left with deep regret."

Almost immediately, in February 1943, the newly formed 3rd Canadian Army Tank Brigade arrived, but consisting largely of familiar faces: the Fort Garrys were back in Headley, and the 1st Hussars were back in Elstead; only the Sherbrooke Fusiliers were new, and Pat Lewis found: "We weren't accepted by the others. They wanted the pubs and the girls and they'd already made the contacts, so we had to go elsewhere for our entertainment." They stayed for 3 months until the end of May 1943 but, with all the 'schemes' that were going on at the time, they were probably living in the area for only half that period.

The 3rd Brigade left Headley at about the time the last armoured regiments were coming over from Canada. Two of these were stationed here: Al Trotter of the 16/22 Saskatchewan Horse recalls: "We arrived in Headley late one summer evening in '43, and were billeted in Nissen huts near an Anglican Church very close to the village" – presumably these were the ones in Rectory Field; and William Curtis of the Essex Regiment remembers: "We were stationed in and around Headley in the fall of 1943 until the spring of 1944." Both these regiments, and the others which came over with them, were disbanded, and their men sent to augment existing regiments.

But earlier, when the 5th Division had arrived here in the spring of 1942, where was the armour? The Straths had only a "few old Lees and a couple of Rams which had just arrived in the third week of March," and the Garrys had "very few tanks" then, according to Harvey Williamson. The full complement for a regiment at the time was supposed to be in the region of 50–60 tanks, and these were eventually delivered in batches over the next few years as the regiments moved around Britain from location to location. In April 1942, however, the tank regiments had arrived, but effectively they had no tanks.

Fort Garry Horse in Aldershot, winter 1941.
There are 84 men and 3 tanks on parade.

Fort Garry Horse with Grant type tanks near Aldershot, early 1942.
There appears to be one tank per squadron here.

Arford and Headley Down
(base map dated 1937, with some later additions)

= Tank Park
= Nissen Huts

Erie Camp

Windmill House

Crestafield

Beech Hill

squadron on Ludshott Common

Showing position of Tank Parks and Nissen Huts 1942–44
(Modern road names in brackets differ from those shown on map)

Billets and Parking Lots

Although the army already owned a number of properties in Headley, others were requisitioned in order to accommodate the hundreds of troops coming into the village. Grace Barnes (née Snow), who lived then as in 1993 down Glayshers Hill, remembers: "My husband had been called up in 1940, so I was here on my own, and they wanted to billet troops on me – I wasn't having that, so I went down the road to my parents' home and lived there." Her house was let to two different families during the war, and suffered cracks in the ceilings due to the constant tank traffic up and down the hill.

Generally the Canadians were moved into empty houses rather than sharing with the local householders. Some of these were up Barley Mow Hill, and others mentioned were *Belmont*, *Hatch House Farm*, *Kenton House*, *Windridge*, *The Mount*, *Beech Hill House*, *Walden* (now *Heathfield*) and *Pound Cottage*. Jim Clark's father worked for the army during the war as a carpenter, though he was a wheelwright by trade, and he used to go round these houses doing repairs. Sometimes the damage was substantial; Sue Allden recalls that *Sunnybank* (by Arford Farm) was almost torn to bits by Canadians billeted there.

Church Gate Stores in the High Street was used as a squadron orderly building, and Canadian troops there added to the wealth of graffiti already in the attic from domestic servants of previous generations.

Graffiti added in Church Gate Stores attic.
It is thought that Trooper D.123094 James L. Desaulnier was
a Despatch Rider (D.R.) with the Fort Garry Horse (F.G.H.).
The date 20th August 1942 was one day after the ill-fated Dieppe raid.

26

In addition, Nissen huts were erected all over the place: in the Rectory Field beside the hedge from the school up to the *Holly Bush*, on the Village Green, on Openfields, in gardens along Barley Mow Hill, in woods behind *The Mount*, in Crestafield (now the Windmill estate), in fields now occupied by Hilland estate, on Cricket Lea in Lindford, and on the edge of Ludshott Common next to Seymour Road. Erie Camp, of course, was a special case – the 66 wood and brick buildings there were for the exclusive use of the prisoners and their guards.

Pat Lewis recalls the NAAFI on Ludshott Common and the two ladies who ran it with great affection: "We didn't have much money and our regiment felt, to some extent, like outcasts – we were the new guys brought into the Division. That was the reason we used the NAAFI so much, and these ladies were marvellous, absolutely marvellous – the army food was pretty good, but we never liked it, and they would supply us with sandwiches and soufflés and things."

Church Gate Stores: Fort Garry Horse 'B' Sqn stores;
Capt Alex Christian leaning against the fence.

Harvey Theobald, in 'A' Squadron of the Garrys, also tells of the joy of supplementary provisions: "To add variety to the monotonous army rations, we were indeed grateful for the greens, in season, provided by the fforde's farm (*Coolgreany*); the green spring onions from Rogers store (now *Crabtree House*) devoured by the troops like candy bars; and milk products from the dairy (*The White House*) run by Percy and May Wilcox.

Grace Barnes remembers there was a cookhouse behind *The Mount*. She had two Labrador dogs which she kept in a big run in her garden, and when they caught the scent of cooking they tore holes in the netting to get out – however, she always knew where to go and find them. The sign "Regimental Butcher" is still to be seen painted inside the door to the garage at *Headley Mount Cottage*, as are the blue lines painted on the wall outside to separate the bins for 'swill only' and 'ashes only'.

27

For young Canadian men seeing life in rural England for the first time, Headley seemed to take on a magical quality. Pat Lewis recalls: "We were amazed at how tidy the people were, how they looked after their environment in those days. You had the guy with the wheel-barrow, the shovel and the brush, and he kept the gullies along the road clear, and he swept up the leaves. You looked out of the window in the morning in Headley and saw flowers all over the place, and what impressed us most was the tranquillity – you'd do guard duty, and from 2 to 4 o'clock in the morning you'd hear all kinds of bird songs as the false dawn came in." Harvey Theobald noted that the sound of the cuckoo was first treated by them as a novelty, but very soon wore out its welcome.

View from Mill Lane of the Holly Bush,
taken by a Canadian soldier, Ralph Howlin

Al Trotter recalls a different sort of attraction: "One evening an NCO and I went for a walk along one of those nice footpaths. The flowers were blooming all over the place. The trees just about covered the path in areas. It was beautiful. Anyway, we came across this tennis court. Two real pretty girls were pushing a lawn mower and they were having a hard time as the grass was pretty high. This NCO volunteered him and me to cut the grass for them. I wasn't keen on the idea, but nevertheless went along with it. We cut grass and trimmed flowers for about an hour, then, lo and behold, a couple of young officers came upon the scene with their tennis gear on. They thanked us, but I had the feeling we were being had. All the rest of the evening I gave this Corporal a hard time, and asked him what we were trying to prove, as we didn't even know how to play the game." *Now then, you Headley locals – own up, who was it?*

When the tank regiments received their tanks, these were often parked near to the troops. Mrs Warner remembers: "You would sometimes find a tank in the corner of someone's garden – they just put down a slab of concrete under overhanging trees, and drove a tank in there." There were

28

tanks parked up Barley Mow Hill and Headley Hill Road, down Beech Hill Road where the scout hut is, along the Grayshott Road opposite Ludshott Common, at Crestafield where the Windmill estate is now, along Liphook Road where Hilland estate is, down in Lindford by the cross roads, in Openfields where the school is now, and behind *Rowley House* in what was known as 'Rogers Field'. *(See maps pp.14, 24, 25 to identify locations, and Appendix I for billeting arrangements of squadrons).*

Jim Clark, who was a schoolboy at the time, lived then as now in Church Lane and remembers the tanks just at the top of his road in Openfields. "They used to take us on the tanks – it was one big adventure – they sat us in the seats. We had Churchills here and then Shermans, and some small tanks we called 'Littlies'". He also recalls being in school one afternoon when the Canadians decided to have a grenade-throwing practice in the Rectory Field: "Old Amos sent us home from school early that day, saying there's no point in trying to teach us with all that noise going on."

"Quite an exciting time for us," he continues. "We used to wander round the tanks up there – they had everything all laid out – I remember seeing a load of revolvers and Sten guns beside the tanks. They were very irresponsible in a way – they used to leave ammunition all over the place, and you could go along and just pick it up – take the bullets, knock the heads off, take the cordite out and make rockets of them."

Cutting from a Canadian Newspaper – Spring 1942
(see photo of Pete Friesen and his brothers p.36)

Fort Garry Horse regiment in Headley, 12 June 1942

*General Montague with Lt-Col Morton on his left
and Maj EB Evans on his right*

*Troopers Kapitany, Livingstone, and Scott
on the fender of their M3 Lee tank*

Encounters with the Locals

The local population were in two minds about their visitors from abroad. Joyce Dickie (née Snow, Grace Barnes' younger sister) worked at the telephone exchange in Bordon and recalls the first Canadian soldiers she met there: "They were all bad ones that they'd taken from prison – I got into contact with them quite a bit and they were really horrible." She used to say this to her mother, but was told: "You shouldn't talk like that, they've come over to help us." Her mother ran dances and social evenings on behalf of the Red Cross in the Village Hall, which the War Office had commandeered. People promised to give a penny a week towards the cost, and Joyce went round the village to collect the pennies every Monday. There were plenty of young Canadian soldiers at these dances, and Joyce met one there who she later married. "So I changed my mind about them eventually," she said.

Many villagers would invite servicemen in for a cup of tea on a more or less regular basis, and others organised small parties for them. "We used to have little parties up on Headley Down and invite the soldiers," Joyce Dickie remembers. "We couldn't get very many in because it was only a little hall (along Fairview Road, now a dwelling). We each used to ask one soldier, and we'd supply cider and crisps – we had some jolly good times up there." Jim Richards told his sister, Betty Roquette, how he would go across from the huts at Crestafield to get fruit and fish & chips from Mrs Eddey, who had open house for the Canadians on Sundays. Mr Eddey also used to run dances.

Some of the Canadians remember the time when Jack and Marjorie Harrison invited them round to their house (at *Reynolds*, Standford Lane) for a corn roast. John Whitton, an officer in 'B' Squadron of the Garrys, recalls: "It was a very North American event. Marjorie was an American by birth, English by education, and had grown the corn at Headley from seed sent to her by her father in Connecticut. It was delicious."

The soldiers held social events of their own. Joyce Dickie recalls: "They used to have parties in Bordon, and come round in a big truck to pick up all the girls. There was so much food, and we were rationed. They had lots of cigarettes with flip-tops, and sweets." On a more formal level, some of the village ladies were invited round by the Canadians for supper evenings. Joyce Stevens remembers going with the rector's daughter and others to *The Mount*, off Barley Mow Hill, where they were given what they assumed to be a typical Canadian meal – heaps of food, and all on one plate. John Whitton recalls the time the 'A' Squadron officers gave a garden party and invited all their neighbours round. "There was tea, sandwiches, punch and other refreshments. One or two of the elderly guests didn't fully realize what the other refreshment really was – their systems weren't accustomed to it and they were helped home with much laughter."

Village men serving in the British forces returned on leave to find Canadians "all over the place" and were not altogether happy about the situation, but the local girls were of a different disposition. As Pat Lewis put it: "They'd been brought up on American movies, and they associated us with the Americans and the great prairies of Canada, and thought it would be marvellous to live out there." Local girls remember being told: 'Marry me – I own a gopher farm back home.' "If I'd been a young Headley village boy I'd have been very uptight about things," said Pat; but he adds, "we fought more among ourselves than we did with the villagers." Tom Webb of the Garrys writes: "I do know that the people of the village were most gracious and friendly to us, and even forgiving, for we were not exactly angels."

The Crown Inn, Arford in 1993

Betty Parker (née Aldred), who lived then as now in *Eashing Cottages*, remembers going down the alley beside *Belmont* with a friend and putting sticks out for doughnuts – the Miss Laverteys used to scold them for it, she says. She was aged about 14 or 15 at the time. "We used to have good fun with their boxes of chocolates and cookies – we'd say 'any gum chum?' and they'd give us a big packet of gum. We used to go up by *The Chestnuts* (now *Hill Cottage*, on Barley Mow Hill), and they'd say 'mend my socks and you'll get some chewing gum,' and we girls used to mend their blooming socks – darn them just for a piece of chewing gum. They were always chewing gum – always."

They also had a reputation for drinking a fair amount. The pubs were very different to Canadian bars – and "they got so wild because they drank here as they never could in Canada – and they had more money than our men," as one local remembers it. The three pubs in Headley seemed to be packed out most of the time. "It wasn't just the troops based in Headley," said Pat Lewis, "we had the Canadian Army women in Bordon plus the laundry (on Broxhead Common) which most of them worked in – for some reason or other they all seemed to be in the pubs at Headley, at least while we were there, so you had to hold onto your glass – if you put it down, it disappeared and you couldn't get another drink.

The Wheatsheaf Inn, 1993 (now demolished)

"Sometimes you couldn't get into the bar – there was a stairway in the first pub as you go down the hill (the *Wheatsheaf*) that went up to the snug – well that staircase, it used to be full – no room inside." He was stationed in the huts on Ludshott Common by Seymour Road, and says he used to do most of his drinking in the *Fox and Pelican* at Grayshott, where it was quieter. Troops from his regiment were also taken by trucks to Haslemere and "dropped by the two hotels" there. More than once he had to walk back when he missed the return lift.

Betty Parker, too, recalls that the pubs were packed. She lived between the *Crown* and the *Wheatsheaf*, and remembers them charging 2/6d deposit on a glass, so her father used to take a jam jar along. Arthur Dean recalls that Mr Smallbone, the landlord of the *Crown*, would get two or three local lads to go round and pick up the glasses, so when the soldiers wanted another drink they had to go and pay their half crown again.

The troops would sit in a row opposite the *Wheatsheaf*, where the phone box is now, and Betty remembers the publican there following them up the road asking for their glasses back, and seeing them drop them on the road in front of him. John Whitton recalls: "I've forgotten the owner's name, but his teenaged daughter was called Jeannie, I believe, and while really too young to be drawing beer for us, she was very good natured and popular with us all."

Harvey Williamson says: "'Old Charlie' played the piano in the *Crown* – not very well, not much more than 'You Are My Sunshine,' but he'd keep playing so long as you put a pint on his piano." Sometimes they'd send out the jeep to find out the opening times of the various pubs – it seemed that one would open as another closed. He admitted that when they went out, the emphasis was on the drinking. Tom Webb, of the same regiment, remembers good times at the three pubs, and "an unforgettable pint of Old at the *Wheatsheaf* after a drinkless trip from Glasgow. I still taste it," he says.

Taken by Alex 'Danny' Getz of the Fort Garry Horse,
outside The Cricketers, Kingsley

Pat Lewis commented that with many Canadians it was the way they drank it which gave them problems with English beer – mixing it up with spirits or drinking whisky chasers. They were also "knocked around a bit" by the old ale which came out in winter time, but Al Trotter says he found his first Mild & Bitter quite potent enough, "much to my sorrow the next morning."

Even those who couldn't get to meet the locals still have their memories of them. Len Carter of the 1st Canadian Parachute Battalion who, after taking a prolonged and unauthorised leave in London, found himself behind the wire of Erie Camp, remembers: "From those days I came away with an impression which has stayed with me all this time. Gazing one day at freedom beyond the wire, I saw this elderly grey haired lady, a stately looking person on a high-seated bicycle pedalling slowly, almost majestically, along the road with a cigarette hanging from the side of her mouth. I believe that if an army convoy had come along it would have pulled over to accord her right of passage, and I thought at the time it was she, not Britannia, who typified the Brits." *Many readers in Headley will have their own ideas as to who this lady might have been.*

Services and Entertainments

The Parish Church at Headley became a garrison church for the Canadian troops in the area, and was later presented by the Canadians with a beautiful silk flag with a maple leaf on it, in grateful memory. Mrs Warner played the organ here for many years, and remembers that the soldiers' service was held an hour or so before the regular village service – and when the villagers arrived, there were complaints from certain Headley residents about the smell of 'wet khaki' lingering in the church.

Non-conformists used to go to the Congregational Chapel off Long Cross Hill, and Betty Parker recalls that a lot of Canadians went there – "I think they liked that kind of service," she said. Pat Lewis, as a Catholic, went to St Joseph's church at Grayshott in whose churchyard 95 of his Catholic compatriots from the First World War lie buried. Others may have attended Mass in Mr Alex Johnston's garage at *Leighswood* along Headley Fields, which he offered for use when petrol rationing made travel to Grayshott increasingly difficult.

The army had requisitioned the Village Hall, and various entertainments were put on here for the troops. (The floor had to be replaced after the war due to the damage caused by the soldiers' boots.) Betty Parker and Jim Clark both remember the cinema shows there, and how the local children would creep into the front in the dark – "they weren't supposed to be there of course." Dances were on Friday or Saturday, with the villagers providing cakes, refreshments and raffle prizes. These were generally happy events, and although the local *Herald* newspaper of the period reported three separate 'incidents' in which Canadian soldiers were brought to court for molesting local girls, this can hardly be considered exceptional over a four year period.

Soldiers stationed away from the centre of the village often went else-where for their entertainment. Those on Ludshott Common tended to go to Grayshott and Haslemere – Pat Lewis, who was in Nissen huts by Seymour Road with the Sherbrooke Fusiliers, says that he never heard of a dance going on in Headley. The only village function he remembers attending in his 3 months here was at Grayshott, where they had a regimental sports day at the playing field just before they left the area, and the ladies put on tea for them.

Those based in Lindford had cinema shows in *Hatch House Farm*, and walked to dances at Liphook Village Hall, according to Pete Friesen of the Garrys 'HQ' Squadron, which was quartered in Nissen huts at Lindford during both visits here – they knew the *Holly Bush*, but otherwise rarely visited the centre of Headley. His elder brother Jack ('Shorty') and younger brother Dave *(see photo)* were with him here. They were all in the Garrys' regimental band, which was the HQ Squadron scout car troop, the Sergeant in charge being the band leader. The residents of Lindford should have heard some fine reveilles!

The Friesen brothers (Jack, Pete and Dave), who were all in the Fort Garry Horse regimental band. This picture was taken in Canada.

Soldiers and civilians alike from Headley used to go to the two cinemas in Bordon during the war: the *Palace* in Deadwater and the *Empire* behind the Post Office (now the sorting office) off Camp Road. Sue Allden remembers catching the bus from the village to the *Empire* and seeing many films there – she remembers it was always full of soldiers, and had that distinctive smell of khaki uniforms about it. Close to the *Empire* was the 'Church of England' club, which also proved popular with servicemen in the area.

'Whitey', the Fort Garry mascot

Villagers such as Katie Warner have fond memories of the Garrys' mascot, 'Whitey' the Collie dog: "He used to lead the regiment to church. They'd bring him in, and he would lie down in the aisle right by the front pew, and would stay there the whole time. If you couldn't see him you wouldn't know he was there – and when the service was over he would get up and lead them out again."

'Whitey' had been smuggled into England in a box under anaesthetic, and was a great favourite with troops and villagers alike. Rod Waples, secretary of the Fort Garry Horse Association, says: "'Whitey' was a Fort Garry Horse member – his Regimental No. was H-26000½ – and he came to us one cold night in the winter of 1939. He appeared on the doorstep, was invited in to warm up, and stayed."

'Whitey', mascot of the Fort Garry Horse regiment

John Whitton remembers: "Whitey lived with 'B' Squadron, and at morning parade time, when the Sgt. Major would shout his orders to "fall in," Whitey would literally herd the men into their various troop formations, all the while barking and rounding up the slow movers. He knew to be quiet when the Sgt. Major was about to give forth with subsequent 'orders', but would then give more barking, just to punctuate the occasion." Ted Brumwell, also of 'B' Squadron, recalls: "He would attach himself to a Trooper as his master for a couple of weeks, then move on to another troop."

Sadly, 'Whitey' was accidentally run over and killed by a truck Tuesday, 28th March 1944, shortly before D-Day, and buried with proper military ceremony at a spot code-named 'Shangri-La' near Fawley in May 1944.

An article in *The Rally* by Frank B Dowd, dated 1st May 1944, tells us more about how 'Whitey' came to be with the regiment:—

"It was on the first route march after the Garrys mobilized that 'Whitey' joined up. The route march took the boys through the west end of the city. Tied to the verandah of one of the houses that they passed was a three-weeks old pup, who strained and tugged on his leash until at last it gave way. Whitey joined his first parade and marched back to barracks.

"That night the owner called for 'Whitey', and took him home. The next day, however, another route march took the boys past 'Whitey's' place of captivity. Again he broke loose and ran away to join the Army. Again his owner called for him, and took him home. Time after time this happened. Finally his master decided that he might as well give in. He presented him to his new friends, and thus 'Whitey' joined the Fort Garry, and was duly attested as the regimental mascot."

'Dad's Army' to the Rescue!

Extract from the personal history of Bob Grant

Bob and other officers from his squadron of the Fort Garry Horse were billeted at 'Long Cross Farm' in April 1942, and he recounts the following amusing tale:—

We would keep our beer supply cool at the bottom of the well in our yard. The beer was put in a pail and lowered about thirty feet into very cold water. Unfortunately, one day the pail tipped over and we lost two dozen very scarce and very precious bottles.

A scheme was devised where I was to be lowered into the well to retrieve the treasure. Sadly, when I was half way down, the wire broke and I landed in the cold water which was about five feet deep, and it was absolutely pitch dark. Other than being surprised, I was unhurt.

"Our palatial home": Long Cross Farm
Maj. Bob Grant, Maj. Owen Atkins, Lt. John Whitton

My fellow conspirators were quite concerned about my well-being (no pun intended). A quick search failed to turn up a ladder long enough or any other suitable piece of equipment that could be used to extricate me from my predicament. One would have thought that a first class Canadian Regiment would provide the necessary tools to solve the problem, but my friends devised the bright idea to call in the local branch of the Home Guard, who rescued me in no time; cold, wet, without the beer, but otherwise unharmed.

What really hurt was that the South Alberta Regiment, which included an old school chum of mine, replaced us in the lines a short time later, and they recovered the beer.

Treats and Recreations

As well as participating in village entertainments, the troops organised their own recreations. The official records of both the Garrys and the Straths mention a full programme of sports competitions, including baseball, boxing, hockey and cross-country running, held between Canadian regiments. 'Slim' Bradford, now living in Hindhead, though not based in Headley at the time, remembers visiting the village to take part in a boxing match. He recalls too the 24-hour gambling schools which "took place in all locations."

The Canadians gave treats to the locals, especially at Christmas time. Katie Warner says: "When the Canadian soldiers realised that sweets and chocolate and everything were so very scarce here, they sent over big boxes of them which were taken to the school and distributed among the children. I'm sure there must be hundreds of children around here who received some of those sweets." They organised Christmas parties at the Village Hall, and gave the Holme School children a party at *Hatch House Farm* in Lindford. "They picked us up in a lorry," Jim Clark recalls, "and at Wellfield Corner we hit another lorry coming the other way – no-one was hurt, but I remember the bang." He also remembers the wooden yacht he was given – "a super little boat with sails and everything."

They arranged parties at Erie Camp for the local Headley Down children, at which they gave out presents made by the prisoners – and some of these are cherished to this day. Grace Barnes still has the lovely doll's cot which her daughter received there. "They were very good at making different things you know," she says, "and the food was alright. It was behind the barbed wire, coils of it – you had to go up into the camp and into one of their recreation rooms, I suppose it was." Mary Fawcett (née Whittle) remembers her disappointment when the gifts were given out in alphabetical order – there were no prams left when they got to her, and she received a small rocking-horse instead.

Some of the 'treats' were somewhat more illicit. Betty Parker remembers her father complaining that they had no sugar one day, only to find a military lorry arriving later with a big bag for him. Others remember a 'black market' going on round the village for cans of petrol and other rationed material.

The Canadians also did their bit to 'dig for victory'. The official record of the Straths tells how "spare time was devoted to the planting of gardens," and mentions that "Squadron-Sergeant-Major Sam Heinrich, thanks largely to a hothouse which he usurped, was able to supply 'A' Squadron with fresh radishes a full week ahead of all the others."

Len Carter too, behind the wire in Erie Camp, was planting Brussels sprouts "and other edible albeit disgusting things" between the buildings there, having "finally managed to escape the 'infernal rectangle' or parade square" because he remembered a little maths from school. The RSM had demanded if there was anyone who could figure out the square area of a triangle – he was the only one to volunteer, and was detailed to help Staff Sgt Williams who was in charge of "planting every available foot in the compound with vegetables." This NCO had to submit a statement to the Commandant showing the total area under cultivation, and hence his need for Len's mathematical skills! Len drew up a coloured plan of the entire compound area under cultivation – which largely consisted of a lot of yellow areas indicating Brussels Sprouts, "one of the dirtiest gastronomical tricks the Belgians ever played on us."

One of Ellis's horses before the War

And finally, we should not forget that there were some particular skills which the Canadians brought with them, as John Ellis discovered one day. He remembers: "The last horse to be used for the delivery of animal feedstuffs at Headley Mill was named *Boxer*. Some pasture land adjoining the mill had been requisitioned to produce cereals under the War Emergency Act, and *Boxer* was needed to haul a trailer to help with the harvesting. We tried to catch him one summer's evening, but without success – he dashed around the field and we found it impossible to get him. A crowd of Canadian soldiers came and leant over the gate to see what was going on, and eventually one of them came into the field and asked if we had a long rope. We produced one – and *Boxer* was lassoed within seconds."

A Few Problems

Given the large number of troops, both British and Canadian, who passed through the village during the war, it is gratifying to find how fond are people's memories of that time, and how few the problems which they now recall. Reactions against the first Canadians stationed at Bordon, mentioned earlier, might have stemmed from the fact that some of the initial 'waves' contained ex-convicts. "If you had six months to go in prison, you could apply for early release to join the army," said Pat Lewis. "To some extent, the army were looking for this sort of person – who was prepared to take chances and to fight. A lot of us went straight from school into the army, so we were high on dreams, but these guys were in jail and used to hard living – it takes a crook to catch a crook, sort of thing – so the army was glad to have them.

"Before you could get into the tank regiments, however, you had to sit an education and an intelligence test." The Sherbrookes started off as a mounted machine-gun regiment, "but then," Pat says, "they decided to make us a tank regiment, and the test they gave us took away nearly half of our people." This didn't necessarily weed out all the rougher elements though, and indeed those who were more 'street-wise' helped the rest of the men in the regiment look after themselves.

The local press, being censored, was very restricted as to the hard facts it could publish, but any case that came to a civil court seemed to be fair game. Thus we read that Canadian soldiers were involved in a number of vehicle accidents: such as the Bombardier driving his Colonel's car at night along the Grayshott straight in October 1940 who "did feloniously kill and slay" a trooper of the 10th Hussars walking along the road outside *Stonehaven*; and the Canadian despatch rider who was killed when his motor bike ran into a 3-ton anti-aircraft lorry crossing the road at Headley Mill in July 1942.

Other reported incidents involved accidental deaths among Canadian servicemen in Headley, such as the soldier who shot his friend while fooling around with a loaded pistol outside *Church Gate Stores* in August 1942. Joyce Stevens, who lives next door in *Suters*, remembers hearing it happen. She also remembers a couple of soldiers arguing over a girl outside the little wooden shops (now the parade of shops) next to the *Holly Bush*. "It ended up with a gang fight and one of them was kicked to death," she said. This was probably the incident recorded in the *Herald* as occurring on 15th March 1943, in which a Canadian soldier was found guilty of manslaughter and given 13 days imprisonment. The judge said it was "one of those cases where death resulted unexpectedly from a blow struck in a fight."

The Strathcona's first fatality occurred on 17th June 1942 when, according to a *Herald* article which was surprisingly uncensored for the time: "Lieutenant Richard Anderson Squires, 2nd Armoured Regiment, Canadian Forces, lost his life as the result of falling from a tank at Ludshott Common. The deceased officer, who was in his 32nd year, was the son of the late Sir Richard Anderson Squires, twice prime minister of Newfoundland." The Straths' official record adds: "He was our only Newfoundlander, and very popular." He was buried in Brookwood Cemetery.

Towards the end of the war, when the Princess Louise's Fusiliers had returned from Italy and were stationed for a short time at the Headley end of Ludshott Common, the body of a 24 year-old Private was found, "in full battle dress but without his cap," in a frozen static water tank underneath an inch of ice. He had arrived at the camp on 30th October 1944, and should have proceeded to Canada with a PoW escort group on 23rd November. Posted as 'absent without leave' on 9th November, his body was not discovered until the beginning of January 1945.

Canadian-made concrete blocks at Ludshott Common dated 25/28 Aug 1941

The *Herald* describes the water tank as "brick, 20ft diameter, 12ft deep and holding 12,600 galls. It was mainly below ground level. Its edges were surrounded by grass which sloped up from the main drive in and a footpath – a rise of about 1ft in 1ft.

The tank was right opposite the NAAFI canteen. The top was in no way protected – wire netting and poles had been removed in September." An open verdict was recorded by the Winchester District Coroner.

Some Memories

For every event which was reported there must have been dozens which remain only in the memories of those involved. Joyce Stevens, right opposite the *Holly Bush*, recalls hearing "an awful kerfuffle at turning out time when Sally Stevens, the landlady, was saying goodnight to everybody as she always did. I remember she was wearing a white blouse, and she'd got blood all down the front of it because one of the soldiers had broken off a bottle or something and cut someone."

Sally is fondly remembered by the troops; as Major Macdougall writes in his *Short History* of the South Alberta Regiment: "We must not forget to mention that 300 lb bundle of good humour, whose only regret was that, while she had played with Canadians in the last war, in this war she could only mother them." He also recalls Christmas here in 1942, when "all ranks enjoyed themselves to the full, and I mean to the full." He continues that: "Apart from a few slight run-ins with our friends the Elgins, who were at Headley Down, the day passed peacefully enough."

Elsie Johnson (née Pearce) was living with her parents in their shop (now closed) in Fullers Vale at the bottom of Beech Hill.

Old Shop in Fullers Vale, 1993

She says: "I can remember one incident on a Saturday night. Mabel and I had come home from work – we often didn't get back till nine – and mum and dad were scrubbing out the shop. We had a plain white wooden floor and stairs, and every Saturday night without fail they were scrubbed. Newspapers were put down, and the lights were on downstairs, though you couldn't see much of them through the shutters, and some Canadians walking back down to the village tried to get in. They thought it was a pub. Father shouted to them that we were shut and we didn't sell liquor, but they climbed the bank on the left hand side, and walked in through the kitchen door. I can see dad now, coming up the stairs with a scrubbing brush in his hand – and with brute force we all pushed these lads out. We didn't know any of them, but they were determined it was a pub and that they were coming in for a drink."

John Ellis at Headley Mill found a different way to deal with such things: "One night after midnight, a party of noisy Canadians, obviously the worse for drink, took a short cut past the mill to get back to Bordon Camp. When they got to the house they stopped just under our window, and created the most frightful din.

Aerial view of Headley Mill, 1955

The house was not then modernised, and each bedroom had a wash hand-stand complete with wash bowl and water jug. I got out of bed, in spite of Dorothy's protestations, eased up the sash window, took the 3 gallon jug of cold water and poured it over them. There was deathly silence. We didn't hear another thing – we didn't even hear them move away."

Betty Parker remembers talking to a Canadian motorcyclist and his pillion passenger outside *Eashing Cottages* in Arford – the passenger decided to get off, but the other drove away. Almost straight away he ran into a lorry at the corner, and was killed. "Those Harley Davidson machines always looked powerful to us," Jim Clark says, "and so did the 'Indians', which were the other motorbikes they used." He too remembers a fatal motorbike accident nearby: "One of them hit a tank by Arford House – went straight into it as he was coming down the hill." *Not a nice place to meet oncoming traffic even now.*

Mary Fawcett, living down Beech Hill at the time, recalls a Canadian on a Harley Davidson crashing through the hedge at the Honeysuckle Lane bend, hitting an electric pole and taking out the whole of the public electricity supply in the area. She also remembers a tank coming along Fullers Vale failing to take the bend at the bottom of Beech Hill and hitting the post box which was then in the gatepost at the bottom of Kenton House drive. *The post box was then moved to its present safer place.*

Joyce Dickie, on her way home from Bordon telephone exchange, where she sometimes had to work until midnight, was walking up Barley Mow Hill when she heard a girl screaming her head off from a piece of common land opposite *Barley Mow House.* "I thought, 'Oh my golly, now what do I do? I can't just walk by and not do anything when somebody's screaming for help.' And yet I had in my mind what was going on, but I didn't know what to do. Anyway, I put on as gruff a voice as I could, and I said, 'What's going on over there?' And this girl came out, and the soldier with her. Well, she was terrified, and I think she'd taken on a bit more than she'd realised. She begged me to take her home, and I thought, what if I meet the fellow when I come back up again? I did go home with her, but that chap plagued me for weeks afterwards – wanted me to go out with him, but eventually he got fed up."

Altogether, Barley Mow Hill seemed to be quite a centre of activity at this time. "The 'provos' were always busy up this road," says Grace Barnes speaking of Glayshers Hill, "because we had an 'interesting' house just round the corner where the telephone exchange is now." Glayshers Hill led from the Provo's quarters in Erie Camp down to Barley Mow Hill. "We didn't dare get out and about in the road much – you kept yourself pretty quiet", she said.

However the Provost Corps themselves, according to *Battle-dress Patrol*, the official war memoirs of the Royal Canadian Mounted Police, felt that: "Despite long years of training and waiting and the consequent boredom, I think it fair to say that our troops were well behaved. Provost units had much less trouble with them than might be thought. We like to think our approach helped; provost men were taught and encouraged to help soldiers who were in trouble – sick, broke or overdue off leave. At times more stern action was necessary when dealing with public disorder and drunkenness, but these causes were surprisingly rare."

Air Raids

While spared the intensity of the air attacks which were hitting Portsmouth and other strategic locations, the residents of Headley nevertheless became all too familiar with the sound of sirens. Joyce Dickie recalls an occasion when it went just as she was due back at work in Bordon. "When the siren went you were supposed to stay put, but on this occasion it was such a long time before we got the all-clear, I said to myself: 'I can't wait here any longer – there's no sign of anything, so I'll go'. Well, I'd just got to Lindford when the planes came over. I was stopped there and had to get down in the pit with the men at the garage. Then it seemed to be alright, so they let me get on my bike and off I went – and I was almost at the cross roads, where the Military Police had an office, when they came over again. The police stopped me – they wouldn't let me go any farther and made me go in with them. I ended up under the billiard table with these men all round me. A bomb fell right on the cross-roads – the people had been evacuated, but an old lady was worried because her little bird was in there and had gone back to get it, and she was killed – the little bird in his cage was alright."

Tom Grisdale, who was in the Home Guard at the time, remembers the same event: "I was out at five o'clock in the evening, on my field down Liphook Road, and we saw the bombs leave the plane. Me and Derek jumped on our bikes and went down. They dropped all by the Fire Station cross roads – and I think the only person that was killed was the turncock's wife – she came out and went down the shelter, then remembered she'd left the canary, ran back to get it, and she just got caught in the middle of it."

He also remembers Canadian soldiers sharing his dug-out in Mill Lane, opposite Churchfields, during air-raids: "We used to get down there at about 6 o'clock in the evening, and regularly this used to be when, as it got dark, the siren would go – and they'd all come out from Bordon and spend the night with us." Betty Parker remembers Canadians from Bordon sheltering in Headley too: "They slept in the woods by *Brontë Cottage* up Barley Mow Hill – you'd see them come up every night with their packs on their backs and their blankets – they'd sleep there, and you'd see them going back in the morning."

Katie Warner recalls: "There were air-raid shelters in the school gardens which had been built there for the school children – I used to go in with them and the teachers – as an extra helper with the little ones, the 5 and 6 year-olds – when there was a warning."

Jim Clark says: "For us, ten and eleven year-olds, an air-raid was just one big adventure – we didn't realise the fact that the Germans were across the channel – we didn't think about that. I remember a German plane coming across here, and they opened at it with the Bren guns on tripods."

On 10th February 1943, according to Marcel Fortier of the Foot Guards, "the nearby town of Bordon was heavily strafed, near misses landing in HQ Squadron area and in No. 1 Squadron Tank Park (probably in Lindford), while hits were made on the walls of the Sergeants' Mess"; and both the 1st Hussars and the Sherbrookes recall that on 8th March 1943 a German raider dropped bombs in the Haslemere area. In a footnote to the latter incident, we are told that one of the pilots shot down had studied English in Haslemere before the war – and the local population did not appreciate his return visit.

Another more mysterious visitor from the sky was reported by Jim Clark. One night he and two other village lads saw quite clearly a lone parachutist dropping across the full moon, to land, he would reckon, on Ludshott Common. He reported this to the authorities, and was visited the next day by plain clothes security men in the traditional trench coats, but never heard any more of it.

However, it was not all one-way traffic up in the air. John Whitton says: "We seemed to be on a direct path between an airfield and targets on the continent, as light bombers frequently flew low overhead in formation. They looked very serious." Al Trotter of the Saskatchewan Horse remembers that in the summer of 1943: "Every evening the RAF bombers would pass over Headley on the way to Germany and occupied countries and return the next morning. The count was not always the same next morning." Jim Clark recalls seeing the Americans, when they started the daylight bombing: "They used to meet almost over here – they came from two directions just as we were walking to school, and they used to fire these red flares – I don't know what that was for, but I remember the sky being full of Fortresses." Tom Webb of the Garrys saw what was rumoured to be an early experimental jet that went overhead pouring black smoke, and aeroplanes '*sans* propellers' from Farnborough were also sighted here by Harvey Theobald.

Tanks Around the Block

"The British tank regiments came first", said Tom Grisdale. "They were all up on Ludshott Common – it was just a sea of mud." Jim Clark remembers these being light tank regiments, with 'Matildas' he thinks. But it is the Canadians who the villagers remember most vividly.

"The first lot of Canadians came without tanks – we thought that was bad enough, but then we had Canadians plus tanks", said Joyce Stevens, echoing the feelings of many residents at the time. The squadrons which were parked in the village and in Lindford had to drive through the village to take part in exercises on Ludshott, Frensham and Thursley Commons. Katie Warner remembers: "It was nothing to go up and find a line of tanks all down the High Street, some of them with their tracks off being repaired."

Ram tank of the Fort Garrys being loaded onto a transporter.
This would have been a familiar sight in Headley.

Pat Lewis recalls driving tanks from Headley to Aldershot when they had to do repairs, and going through the lanes to Farnham. "They specialised in tanks at Aldershot, while Bordon was more for the other vehicles", he said. Katie Warner recalls: "They widened our roads for us considerably – especially Mill Lane – it's difficult to imagine it now, but it used to have quite high banks each side going down the hill. But when two tanks met on the hill, nobody was going to stop and go back – and so they each carved into the bank." She remembers the resulting mud at the top of Mill Lane, by the chestnut tree. It was so bad that when her six year-old son slipped and fell there on their way to church, she had to take him straight home to clean him up, and missed the service.

"If you look around the area now you'll find concrete in the oddest spots", she continues, "maybe in somebody's garden – and there's a bit along the Liphook Road just outside *Littlecote*, where they used to turn to go into the field, in what is now Hilland Estate. Where they were turning on this same spot all the time, they scooped out the road blocking the ditch – so they had to put in this big slab of concrete which allowed them to turn more easily."

Two instances of Canadian concrete still remaining in the village: at Headley Hill Road and at the entrance to Headley Fields

Concrete slabs put down to assist tank movements can still be seen in many other parts of the village: for example, at the sharp corner of Churt Road at Hearn Vale, by the scout hut up Beech Hill Road, at various places along Headley Hill Road, and at the entrance to Headley Fields. According to David Whittle, parts of Carlton Road (as far as the dip) and Seymour Road were made up for tanks to go along and there was a Tank Repair Shed in the middle of Ludshott Common. "Just inside the fence of the school grounds at Openfields, there's concrete still under the grass", Jim Clark says. "They tried to break it up afterwards, but it must be nearly three foot thick – they couldn't touch it, so they just put earth over it – and of course if you get a hot summer now, that grass all dies off first."

"There was a tank shed by where the scout hut is now", Mary Fawcett recalls, "with several tanks parked near it, and there was always a guard standing there, day and night." There were also tank parks laid down opposite Ludshott Common along the Grayshott straight, according to Pat Lewis. At each of these, up to three tanks would run in onto concrete slabs arranged in a 'trifurcated' pattern, hidden under the trees which were there at the time. From these parks the tanks had only to cross Grayshott Road to get to the training area on the Common. This at least saved them from having to drive through the village.

Many residents remember the incident when a tank ran into the side of a house in Arford. The house *(see photograph below)*, since demolished during post-war development, stood at the narrowest part of Arford Road just down from the junction with Long Cross Hill. It had been built with a rounded corner, and according to Katie Warner, "they had a go at that rounded corner more than once." Betty Parker, who lived close by, said that the husband of the lady living there was away in the Navy at the time. "She was Irish, and flew out of doors demanding a guard until it was repaired. He stayed on duty outside there with a rifle at night for several weeks." Sue Allden, who supplied the photograph of the house, recalls the lady telling the tank driver he "couldn't drive a wheelbarrow."

Arford. The house in the foreground (now demolished) was hit by the tank. Eashing Cottages (background) were among those flooded (p.58)

Joyce Stevens (née Suter) remembers that the tanks "kicked up at the back when they started off", and more than once demolished different parts of their garden wall in the High Street. She still has one of the forms from the Canadian Claims Commission, proposing to pay £10 for "damage to stone wall by unidentified C.M.V." on 19th November 1943.

In fact the bill from Johnson & Sons of Liphook for repairing the wall came to £12, so the Suters were £2 out of pocket on this occasion.

Harvey Theobald recalls that their C.O. had ordered that any crew damaging walls, etc, would be responsible for repairing same within 48 hours. "The walls near the entrance to 'A' Squadron tank park and the narrow bridge at Lindford came in for a lot of special attention. Most of our tank crews soon became very proficient as stone masons!"

Sue Allden says the wall by the road shown in her photograph of Arford was "continually being knocked down by tanks", and confirms the report in a contemporary Parish Magazine which mentions the 1914–18 War Memorial being hit and damaged by an army vehicle. *The Memorial was subsequently moved back from the road after the war to its present position, in order to protect it from traffic.*

Headley War Memorial between the wars
when it projected into the road

Pat Lewis remembers how he once hooked a woman off her bicycle – though not in Headley: "I had a recovery tank, with plenty of room, but I misjudged the width, and at the side of the tank there were booms which hit her. She and the bike went over, but thank God there was road works going on, and she landed in a pile of sand there." No wonder veterans tell the tale that the last vehicle in a tank convoy was always the regimental paymaster, who paid out for damage caused along the way.

South Alberta Regiment with RAM tanks in England, 1943.
Tac sign of 45 indicates a Recce Regiment.

An officer of the Calgary Tanks putting the finishing touches on the Tac
markings of a Churchill tank, England, May 1942.
By the vehicle name you can tell that this is an 'A' Sqn vehicle.

See also photos on pages 23, 48 and 56.

Vehicle Identification

Each tank carried a squadron sign and tank number painted on the turret for identification. "I remember the squadron signs", says Jim Clark. "There were squares, circles, diamonds and triangles on the turret – and the squares were parked up here in Openfields. I can remember in the evenings, we were by the *Holly Bush* when all the tanks were coming back up from Bordon, and we looked to see which ones came down our road and which went elsewhere – and when we saw the ones with the squares on we said, 'They're our lot', and sure enough they turned down our way." According to convention in both the British and the Canadian army, the diamonds signified HQ Squadron, and the triangles, squares and circles belonged to A, B and C Squadrons respectively.

Other official identification marks included the *Formation* and *Tactical* signs on the front and rear of each vehicle. The Formation sign for the Canadians was a maple leaf superimposed on a rectangle of the relevant Division's colour – green for the 4th, and maroon for the 5th Armoured Division, and so on. The Tactical (or 'Tac') sign was a number denoting the 'seniority' of the regiment within the Brigade. Conventionally for tanks, this was normally '51', '52' or '53'. Thus, for example, the Foot Guards, as senior regiment in the 4th Brigade *(see Appendix III)*, had a Tac Sign of '51', while the Garrys, second in the 2nd Brigade, would display '52'. Reconnaissance ('Recce') regiments, such as the South Albertas became after they left Headley, displayed '45'. *Other numbering systems existed – for example it can be seen that the 'Tac' sign of the Calgarys at Dieppe was '175'.*

Tanks were also given names according to a convention which varied from unit to unit. Sometimes they were chosen to start with a letter relevant to the Regiment's name: for example all tanks of the Foot Guards carried names beginning with the letter 'F' (Marcel Fortier's tank was 'Fitzroy'); whereas in the Straths and certain other regiments, the names began with the letter of the squadron: A, B or C.

But identification marks shown in photographs, even where the censor has let it through, are not always to be trusted. Pat Lewis recalls: "Wherever we were stationed, we were involved in 'away activities', loaded on tank landing craft, doing fake runs here and there – up to Wales, up to Scotland and then back. We didn't realise at first, but the

'Scam' was on as well – we were taken down the road and they'd tell us to change the lettering on the tank, or something. We'd think, 'What stupid thing's this? We've just done that'. But it was all trying to screw up the German intelligence."

Whereas the Calgarys arrived with British 'Matilda' and then 'Churchill' tanks, all subsequent Canadian regiments here used the American M3 'Grant', M4 'Sherman' or Canadian 'Ram' types. The *Grants* were relatively old-fashioned, and noted for having their main gun 'sponson-mounted' in the body of the tank rather than in the turret *(see sketch opposite)*. This gave them a very limited angle of fire unless you turned the whole tank, and they were eventually replaced by Shermans which did not suffer from this problem. The *Sherman* became the main battle-horse of the Canadians during the Normandy campaign, and was usually powered by dependable twin Diesel engines. *See Grant and Sherman specifications in Appendix IV.*

However, the *Ram* was probably the tank seen most in Headley *(see photo p.48)*. It was a Canadian manufactured version of the Sherman, of all-welded construction, powered by an aeroplane engine running on 100% octane petrol, and is said to have taken its name from the ram on the family crest of General Worthington, the 'father' of Canadian armoured forces. These tanks were relatively fast, but only did 1 mile per gallon with a maximum range of some 100 miles, and also required a great deal of maintenance on their engines. Their protective armour was not very heavy – the Garrys discovered on visiting the Linney Ranges in Wales that a shot from their 2 pounder main armament would go right through them. They were used for training and eventually replaced by 'real' Shermans for operational armoured work, but the changeover was not complete until April 1944 – just 2 months before D-Day.

Silhouettes of tanks used by the Canadians in Headley

Matilda

Churchill

Ram

Exercises and Inspections

While the tank regiments were here, they took part in any number of exercises. As Pat Lewis put it: "Headley was the ideal place to get yourself orientated with your tanks to the English countryside. Later, we were involved in what they called 'schemes' as we were moved around the country prior to D-Day. The British army, often the Home Guard, fought you in mock battles and they gave us a hard time throwing mattresses over the tanks so the driver couldn't see, and so forth. We had to get through towns and countryside as we would see it in France – trying to use tanks in roads where there's hedges all over the place and you can't see what you're doing. But basically we came to Headley to learn how to handle the tanks."

Harvey Theobald recalls that they used 'A' Squadron tank park[†] as a primary area to train new drivers. "Once they became proficient within its confines, our main training could be concentrated on Ludshott and Frensham Commons – which became very busy at times considering that these somewhat small areas had to be shared by three regiments."

Marcel Fortier of the Foot Guards remembers: "Convoy and harbouring schemes occupied much of the time. During the first of these hasty harbour changes it was soon discovered to be not the proper training area, but the private property of the Right Honourable David Lloyd George!"

Individual regiments were inspected during their time here by a number of dignitaries and various Generals, but in April 1942 the 5th Canadian Armoured Division as a whole was inspected by the King and Queen on Frensham Common. Pete Friesen of the Garrys has a picture from a Canadian newspaper showing him with his kit laid out for inspection just prior to the visit (see photo p.29). He remembers thinking that the King looked very ill and white – 'not real'. The official record of the Straths tells how they were wearing their new Maroon patches for the occasion, with 'L.S.H.' inscribed on them, but the King suggested the letters might be confused with other regiments, and recommended they should be changed to 'Ld.S.H.' – which was duly done.

Tanks based in the Headley area used Frensham, Thursley, Hankley and Ludshott Commons for training, as did those based in the Elstead/Tilford/

[†] Now the location of Badgerswood Surgery

Milford area. The 1st Hussars noted that at one time: "The brigade was awaiting repairs to be completed on Ludshott Common before beginning to fire Browning practices at moving targets." They also did tank firing on the 30 yd Conford ranges.

But tanks were in short supply. In the *History of the 1st Hussars*, it states that around June 1942 "the number of our [Ram] tanks never exceeded 18, and the necessary 100 hour inspection of the radial engines meant that several tanks were always off the road for maintenance." It continues by saying that: "The problems were accentuated by the fact that the tanks arrived in England without wrenches and tools, so needing a continual improvisation of the required articles."

*Ralph Howlin (centre, with a 'proper' Sherman tank) of an unknown
Canadian Regiment which was based in Headley during WW2*

Nearly a year later than this, things had not improved much. In early 1943, Pat Lewis remembers sharing the few Ram tanks the Sherbrookes had between their four squadrons: "When we didn't have the tanks, we would use pieces of timber with a centre piece and a rope, and you hung that over your neck, and the group commander was behind with a piece of rope in his hand, and we used to run round Ludshott Common acting as a tank to learn the commands."

One time when he did have a tank to drive, "it was a clapped out Grant, and it broke down in a gully on Ludshott Common. The spares took 3 days to arrive, and we had to stay with the tank until then." By the end of May 1943, the supply of Rams had improved somewhat, and the Sherbrookes were able to transport 'all 49 tanks' when they moved out of the area to go to Worthing.

Al Trotter of the 16/22 Saskatchewan Horse recalls that they started to receive tanks from Bordon when they arrived in the summer of 1943, only to find the regiment was to be broken up. He transferred to the British Columbia Regiment (28th Armoured) and did his armoured training with them around Brighton and Tunbridge Wells.

Floods and Fires

Despite complaints from the regiments of insufficient vehicles, enough tanks were in evidence for the commons to suffer serious loss of vegetation through their movements during the war. Comments from villagers and servicemen sum it up: "Ludshott Common was absolutely barren except for the bigger trees – it was as bare as could be" – "… just a sea of mud where the tanks were – it was so muddy they had duck boards for the troops to walk on where the tanks had cut it up – not a bit of green or anything" – "… it was the tanks and the lorries and what not, going backwards and forwards, that killed the heather and everything" – "… it was just like a rice field – churned up the entire common – no vegetation left on the common at all" – "Ludshott Common was desecrated by the time we'd gone." Jane Durham recalls the common was polluted with oil. At the end, in April 1945, the Ludshott Common Committee reported: "The restoration of the common to anything resembling its pre-war state will be an uphill task which the committee view with great anxiety."

Aerial photo of the east end of Ludshott Common in Sept 1946.
Note complete lack of vegetation to the left.
[Grayshott Hall at top of picture – Superior Camp to right]

57

Those of us lucky enough to live near that Common now, more than 50 years on, know that thanks to the dedicated work of the National Trust, it is once again a glorious habitat for heathland flora and fauna. But during the war years, with nothing growing there to absorb the water, heavy rains ran straight off, down Pond Road and into Arford causing major flooding. Pat Lewis noticed the results of it: "By the time we arrived in Headley (February 1943), the road near the *Wheatsheaf* was a sea of sand washed down there with all the rain."

The water came across the bottom of Beech Hill and down Fullers Vale by Pearce's shop. Elsie Johnson recalls: "We had such terrible floods in October 1942, a particularly wet period – it just came down the full width of Pond Road like a river – it went past our shop and washed the garden of Rose Cottage away – the high kerb was built after that *(see photo p.43)* – the water was up to the second stair in the shop. That was the first time – after that it flooded more often." Tom Grisdale remembers going down Beech Hill one morning after it had flooded overnight, and right opposite Elsie Johnson's shop the water was still deep, and there were "all these tench that had been washed down off the common flopping about in the road." Sue Allden recalls buses were diverted down Barley Mow Hill when Fullers Vale flooded badly, and Mary Fawcett remembers cycling along Fullers Vale each morning to catch the No.6 bus at Bordon for Petersfield, where she went to school: "It was nothing to come home and find it flooded along Fullers Vale."

"It really was bad", said Katie Warner, "I went to the fish shop (also a chip shop, run by the Jelphs) in Arford one morning, and the fishmonger's wife said, 'Have you seen the flooding? You should go down and have a look'. So I walked down as far as Eashing Cottages and the front door of the lowest house was wide open and the water was up to the second step of the stairs – flooded to that depth. Not funny for the people. Every house there was flooded – plus others lower down."

There were times, however, when a spot of water might have been welcome. The 1st Hussars, stationed in the Elstead area, were called out on the night of 9th May 1942 for fire fighting duties on 'Grayshott Common'; and in the *History of the Sherbrooke Regiment* it notes that: "On the afternoon of the 19th May [1943] the unit practised tank-infantry co-operation on Ludshott Common, training which did not occur as planned, because the infantry were chiefly occupied in extinguishing fires started by their mortars."

On a lighter note, Tom Webb of the Garrys writes: "While having an after-duty game of volleyball, our squadron was informed there was a grass fire somewhere and that the Duty Sgt was on his way. Everyone vanished so quickly that the ball was still in the air when he arrived. Being good soldiers, no-one ever volunteered!"

Erie Camp

There were four Canadian camps locally each named after one of the Canadian Great Lakes: Huron and Ontario Camps were on Bramshott Common near to the Portsmouth Road, Superior Camp[†] was at the Grayshott end of Ludshott Common (the concrete road and footings are still very much in evidence there), and Erie Camp was at Headley Down, in the area now occupied by Heatherlands estate.

Of these four, Erie Camp was the 'odd man out', being used exclusively as a military detention centre for Canadian servicemen. "Here we gathered both the casual, happy-go-lucky offenders, and the really bad actors of the army", as the official record of the Provost Corps puts it.

The villagers have many stories to tell of the 'provos' and the prisoners. Betty Parker says: "Whenever anyone escaped, the siren would go and the Provos would be down through the woods with their sticks and red armbands looking for them. This seemed to happen quite often." Grace Barnes, who lived quite close to the Camp remembers: "They often used to get out over the wire – they threw their blankets over the top – and they'd go down into the woods. You used to find bundles of prison clothes down there, and I've always been wondering – someone outside must have been helping them, because what did they wear?" Mary Fawcett remembers seeing prisoners on the run as she picked potatoes in the *Land of Nod* with David, her brother. "They would tear off their trouser legs and throw away their jackets", she said, in order to get rid of the red rings marking them as convicts.

Tom Grisdale says: "I remember when I was on leave, a prisoner had escaped and he got on the bus at Beech Hill Garage. The 'Red Caps' jumped on to arrest him, but the conductor wouldn't let them – he said 'you can't touch him on here – you can have him when he gets off'. So they followed the bus with a jeep and when he got off at the terminus in Haslemere they took him." He adds: "I didn't realise that they couldn't touch him on a public bus." He also recalls: "Some days you'd be on the bus going up towards Grayshott, and the Military Police would be out there seeing prisoners onto the bus when they'd finished their detention."

[†] See aerial photo, p.57.

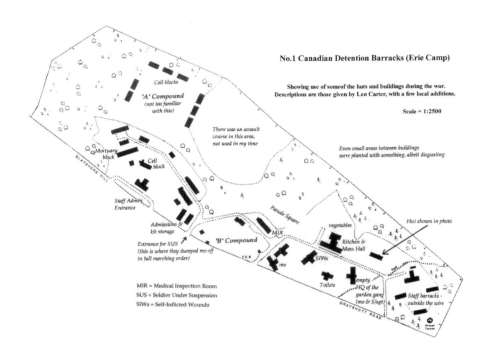

No.1 Canadian Detention Barracks (Erie Camp)

Showing use of some of the huts and buildings during the war.
Descriptions are those given by Len Carter, with a few local additions.

Scale = 1:2500

Cell blocks

'A' Compound
(not too familiar
with this)

There was an assault
course in this area,
not used in my time

Even small areas between buildings
were planted with something, albeit disgusting.

GLAYSHERS HILL

Mortuary
block

Cell
block

Staff Admin
Entrance

Admissions &
kit storage

Entrance for SUS
(this is where they dumped me off
in full marching order)

'B' Compound

MIR

Parade Square

vegetables

Hut shown in photo

Kitchen &
Mess Hall

SIWs

TCB

me

Toilets

empty
HQ of the
garden gang
(me & S/sgt)

Staff barracks
outside the wire

GRAYSHOTT ROAD

MIR = Medical Inspection Room
SUS = Soldier Under Suspension
SIWs = Self-Inflicted Wounds

*Hut on Erie Camp after the war
(see arrow on map above).*

*Mrs Callaghan (later Mrs Wells)
with her daughter Kathleen.*

*Another picture of the huts in Erie
Camp in use after the war –
probably in the 1960s*

See pp.16/17 for pictures of the original construction of the Camp

Servicemen in the area were told to keep away from Erie Camp, "and we did", according to Pat Lewis. However, since it was on the route between Ludshott Common and the village, they could hardly fail to notice it. "We passed the gate and saw the MPs and the guys who came out with them when they took them on a run – forced route marches and things like that." Pete Friesen remembers seeing prisoners from the Detention Centre having to run at the double as soon as they came out of the gates. "The truth is", said Pat Lewis, "we didn't want to go in there not so much for being penned up, but you lost your money – that was the biggest worry – not only did you lose your money while you were in there, but it was also taken off your pension at the end of the war."

One serviceman who did see the inside of Erie Camp for three months in late 1944 was Len Carter, mentioned earlier. On discharge from No.10 Canadian General Hospital at Bramshott, having just won £40 in a game of dice, he decided to turn east and visit London instead of turning west to rejoin his regiment at Bulford. On returning 37 days later he was court-martialled and sent to 1st Canadian Detention Barracks, as Erie Camp was officially called. See p.62/63 for some memories of his time in there.

According to Len it had two compounds for prisoners, A and B, where A was for second offenders and incorrigibles, and B for the first offenders. Compound A, towards the northern end of the camp, consisted of concrete cell blocks. *Villagers remember the problems these caused after the war when the council tried to remove them. "They had an awful job – tried knocking them down and everything – even used explosives, but in the end they were covered up, not removed."*

Compound B consisted of wooden and brick buildings, as did the staff barracks at the south-eastern end of the camp. According to locals, the camp had "huge big gates and rolls of barbed wire" at the main entrance (where Larch Road goes in now) and an observation tower with a searchlight on it. There were offices just inside for admission of prisoners and kit storage. Villagers also remember a water tower, which remained for some time after the war standing opposite Wilson's Road – having survived being burnt in a riot – and some recall a second being down at the Glayshers Hill end.

There was a parade ground at about the point where Maple Way now meets Larch Road, and a large natural depression nearby (where the playing field is now) which Len Carter says had been used as an assault course, though not in his time. Paula Wadhams remembers she called it the 'bomb crater' – it had trees growing in it, and they used to get their Christmas trees from there. After the war it was used by the Council as a Refuse Tip and filled to its present level.

Discipline in the camp was strict and living conditions spartan. As the records of the Provost Corps put it: "One field punishment camp commanding officer said it was his plan to make it so tough that his customers from the front line units would rather go back and stay there than return to his care." He was not talking about Erie Camp, but Len Carter's recollections make it clear that much the same principle applied there. Len says he has never remembered any of the Provost staff there with enmity – "they had a job to do" – but riots took place in the camp at other times when he was not there, during which it seems a few old scores were settled. According to Dot Myers, the prisoners once made the Colonel in charge march up and down with heavy packs on his back.

Jim Clark says: "I can remember going up there when they'd rioted and the whole camp was surrounded by Canadian troops, about four or five deep, like a big wall round it. My father worked for the army as an unofficial locksmith, sort of self-taught, and quite a lot of them had smashed the locks of the cells so they couldn't get out or in – he had to go there and repair them. Quite a big thing, the riot – quite a serious thing."

There was also a "massive break-out" around VE Day. Katie Warner says a lorry was used to charge the gates – "I don't know how they got hold of the lorry, but I do know that some of those prisoners came down to the Village Green and spent the night in the two air-raid shelters in the school garden. We had a big bonfire on the Green that night and some of these prisoners were mingling with us there and admitting that they'd just come out – I think at the time people didn't believe them, but apparently it was so, and it wasn't long before the military police were around collecting them up. I think their stay outside was rather short-lived."

Anthony Vella of the Royal Canadian Electrical & Mechanical Engineers had been sent to 'Headley Detention Barracks' in 1944 to be a part of a rehabilitation programme for prisoners charged with 'Self-inflicted wounds' (SIW), who were "serving 2 yrs detention and facing a subsequent dishonourable discharge." He says: "The programme was designed to teach a trade (I was in charge of the welding school) during their incarceration, and if successful, and if they volunteered to return to their unit and the front, then the dishonourable discharge was withdrawn." Relating to the events described above: "I am happy to say that this re-hab programme was very successful and that during the riots in this camp, when almost everyone was running amok and vandalizing property and manhandling officers and staff, our 'students' did not take part."

Len Carter's memories of his time in Erie Camp

While serving with the 1st Canadian Parachute Battalion in 1944, I spent three months as a soldier-under-sentence (SUS) in Erie Camp Military Detention Centre. Because my offence was not 'refusing to jump' I was permitted to retain my maroon beret, but being the only one with this distinctive headgear, it was not always a blessing. Whenever there was a *merde* detail the cry was, "That man with the red hat!"

The Commandant of the place was a little Scot who strutted about in his trews and Glengarry, and who had a penchant for ordering that all the windows in the hut be flung open on the coldest of days. He had won the VC during WWI so I suppose he had earned the right to freeze those military culprits in his charge.

Conversation between SUS was forbidden except for that short daily spell on the parade square when you were formed up in two ranks – 'Front rank – about turn. Ten minutes – talk.' You might find that your Tête-à-tête partner was a soldier from a French speaking regiment, who was still upset about that business on the Plains of Abraham, but any conversation was better than endless silence ...

There was a locked box of books in the centre of the hut, and we were allowed to read for an hour in the evening. I applied to see the Commandant about purchasing a couple of books so as not to waste the time, but this VC-winning red-faced gentleman bellowed: "You are not here for an education, you are here for punishment."

We probably spent most of our time looking for cigarette butts, which we could furtively smoke by pretending we were stoking one of the two Quebec heaters in the hut, blowing the smoke into the open door, or we could turn up the shower very hot to create a lot of steam and stand at the back of the stall to hurriedly inhale a combination of smoke and steam.

There were two Provost bodies sitting at a table in the middle of the hut at all times – they all had to be addressed as 'Staff' even those who were only privates – and some of them had keen noses. Caught smoking and you existed on bread and water for a few unenjoyable days. "On the ding" was a cute Provost euphemism for 'on charge'.

I believe the 'fast food' concept originated at Headley. I've forgotten the exact number of minutes we were allowed to finish our meal, but if you weren't a fast eater you could often leave the Mess Hall very hungry. Mother may have told you to chew each mouthful at least ten times, but in your letter home you told mother she was out of touch with the real world. Just inside the door was the table where those sentenced to bread and water had their frugal repast.

They say you could tell a Headley graduate by his foot drill – he had that certain Headley stomp, as if there was something evil on the parade square that he was trying to stomp to death. I finally managed to escape the 'infernal rectangle' because I remembered a little maths from school – one morning the RSM demanded if there was anyone who could figure out the square area of a triangle. These requests in the army are pretty tricky and you have to be careful, but I was willing to try anything to get off the 'strutting ground' and I hesitantly raised my hand – the only one to do so. "Right that man with the red hat go with Staff Sgt Williams."

It seems that the S/Sgt was in charge of planting every available foot in the compound with vegetables, and had to submit a statement to the Commandant showing the total area under cultivation, (multiply the length by half the base of the triangle for the number of square feet). With that bit of magic I became the S/Sgt's trusted assistant, mathematician and graphic artist. By drawing up a coloured plan of the entire compound area under cultivation I became the darling of the cultivation gang which consisted of the S/Sgt and myself.

When my kids in later years wanted to leave school early I told them to hold on at least until they had learned how to work out the square area of a triangle, that one day that knowledge might come in handy.　ᓇᓇᓇ

Notes on the commissioning of Erie Camp

No.1 Road Construction Coy RCE (AF) – War Diary

27 May 1941

0630 Fairly warm but cloudy.

0900 Troops loaded in trucks, under a heavy shower of rain.

0930 Departed from Haig Lines. Arrived at Ontario camp at 1045 hrs.

... 30 ORs of 'D' Section detailed to join work party of Lieut JS Parker at Erie Camp.

28 May 1941

OC made a tour of inspection of work parties at Tweedsmuir Camp, Ontario Camp and Erie camps (and again the next day).

According to Len Ford, 'C' Coy of 2nd Bn RCE must have built the huts between Apr 17th and July 14th 1941. His 6th Fld Coy RCE, 7th Brigade, 3rd Cdn Infantry Division arrived July 16th 1941 (see 'Sewer Rats' photos on pp.16/17) and moved out on October 12th 1941.

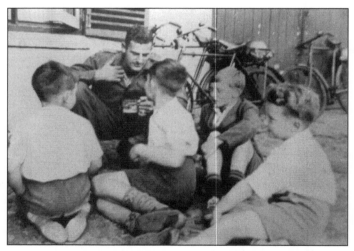

Len 'Henry' Ford talking to boys outside Frensham Pond Hotel, 1941

No.5 Cdn Construction Coy, RCE

Information from Stan Williams:

Arrived at New Martinique barracks at Bordon on the night of 29 July 1941.

Training and construction work were started immediately and the HQ was set up at Whyte Camp, Bramshott on 16 Aug 1941. One detachment started working on the Detention Barracks at Headley and another at Thursley Camp.

The War Establishment of a Construction Coy at this time was 517 ORs and 10 Officers. It was found, however, that there was a deficiency in some trades, so that a Special Increment of 9 Bricklayers, 5 Plasterers, 30 Concreters and 9 Pioneers was added to the establishment. This brought the total up to 570 ORs and 10 officers.

Further work on Headley Detention barracks in 1943.

Lorne Scots – War Diary

Tuesday 2 Dec 1941

0745 Parade of personnel proceeding to Erie Camp, Headley as per Pt.1 Orders Appendix 1.

0910 5 officers, 1 WO, 13 Sgts and S/Sgts, and 101 other ranks and 1 civilian (Cdn Treasury) entrained on special train W630 at Beeston Castle station, Cheshire for Haslemere as per movement Order #33, d/l Dec 41, appendix 3

The train was due to arrive at Haslemere at 1442 hrs but owing to switching at three points was late, arriving at Haslemere at 1515 hrs.

Transport was supplied by RCASC Holding Unit. Personnel were loaded on trucks and transported to Camp in quick time arriving at Erie Camp at approx 1630hrs. The advance party under Major Carson of the Lorne Scots Coy No.1 Cdn Gen Holding Unit had camp well in hand and the men were guided to their quarters and had a good picture of the camp in a very short time.

As soon as the baggage party and office equipment began to arrive the Orderly Room, Pay office and Mail Room began to function as the situation was well in hand and well organized.

Wed 3 Dec 1941

No parades today. Everyone settled down and placed on fatigues. Coy Office, Pay Office, Transport, QM, Transport, Medical Office, Treasury Office and Orderly Room functioning first thing in the morning.

Staff parade held at 0840 hrs and all personnel concerned given an idea of the size of the camp. Everyone seems to be well satisfied as to the layout.

Transport arrived this evening from Oulton Park Camp bringing some equipment left up to the last minute.

Everyone settled and fatigues have been well organized. No air raid warning today. Weather ... fair and cool.

Thurs 4 Dec 1941

No parades today. Lt Col Winfield (AMD2) and Lt Col Sutherland visited the camp this morning. There is some talk of the Unit moving to Tweedsmuir Camp, Thursley and from information received unit is to be in new camp by Thursday 12 Dec 1941.

Telephone message received from CMC Dispersal Wing, Bordon, that a draft of 2 officers, 4 WOs and Sgts and 40 other ranks who are to return to Canada would arrive at 1000 hrs Friday 5 Dec 1941. All concerned warned and everything is being prepared to receive the morning draft.

No air raid warning today. Weather cool.

Notes on the later military use of Erie Camp

The War Office, London, 31st July 1946

To: Headquarters, Southern Command
No.1 Military Prison and Detention Barrack – change of location

1. No.1 Military Prison and Detention Barrack will close at Reading on 7th August 1946 and will reopen at Erie Camp, Headley Down, Hants for the reception of soldier under sentence, on 8th August 1946.
2. The telephone number at Headley Down is Headley 2174 [actually Headley *Down* 2174] and the nearest railway station Haslemere (Southern Railway) approximately 8 miles from Erie Camp. A half-hourly bus service, direct to the detention barrack, operates outside Haslemere station.
3. Soldiers under sentence will be committed to the Military Prison and Detention Barrack, Headley Down, strictly in accordance with its classification as a Group 'C' establishment ...

14/6/48 Circular UM re closing down of Headley Down, July 1948

1. Will you please issue official instructions for No.1 Military Prison and Detention Barrack, Headley Down to complete disbandment by the 26th July 1948.
2. Consequent on the closing down of No.1 MP&DBk, it is necessary to expand No.12 Military Prison and Detention Barrack at Shepton Mallet, which is at present staffed to accommodate 210–300 soldiers under sentence.
3. Will you therefore issue the necessary instructions for this unit to re-organise on HE V/1609/2 to accommodate 301–400 soldiers under sentence – reorganization to take effect from the 26th July 1948.

The Regiments in Action

When the Canadian regiments rolled out of Headley, they passed out of sight of the villagers, but not out of mind. With the strict censorship during the war it was difficult if not impossible to know how individual units were faring, and while this book is not intended to cover events which occurred outside Headley in any great detail, it will interest a number of people to know where the troops eventually went:

The Tragedy of Dieppe

On 19th August 1942, a force consisting mainly of the 2nd Canadian Infantry Division mounted a sea-borne raid on Dieppe. In this they were supported by the Calgary Regiment, using the Churchill tanks which had been issued to them in Headley the previous year. The purpose and timing of the raid remains controversial, and many pages of analysis and comment have since been published on it.

Essentially it seems to have been designed as a test of the Allies' readiness to take a French port and the German's readiness to defend it. There was no intention to follow up with a full-scale invasion at the time; the orders were to take and destroy key objectives in the area, and then execute an orderly withdrawal. In the event, it was a disaster. Every tank that landed was lost, and over 65% of the 5,000 Canadians involved were either captured or killed.

Barbara Boxall's Canadian cousin, Ralph Spencer, who was billeted in Headley during the war, landed in Dieppe and was one of the lucky ones to return. Survivors were given 48 hours leave afterwards to recover. In a taped message sent to Barbara in 1979, he told her: "I managed to get invited to Buckingham Palace for a decoration, which amazed me, and I'm still trying to figure out what happened." Apparently it was for shooting a German sniper who was causing problems there.

He went back to France on D-Day, at H-Hour on Juno Beach, with the Regina Rifle Regiment, and was almost immediately wounded in the legs by machine gun fire. After "quite a few operations" and a long period of convalescence in England, he returned to the continent in time for the war to end while he was in Germany.

About four weeks after the raid, the Germans dropped propaganda leaflets over Headley. Sue Allden and Jim Clark both kept copies *(see p.20)* which they picked up then. These show photographs of the wrecked Churchill tanks, and of dead, wounded and captured soldiers – some recognisable as men who had been in the village not so long before.

In passing, it has become almost a legend in Headley that the tanks 'suddenly left' the village to go on the Dieppe raid; but, as mentioned, the Calgary Regiment had moved away from the area some eight months previously and, according to their 'short history', were not stationed here again. However the Fort Garry Horse and Lord Strathcona's Horse regiments <u>did</u> leave the village suddenly at that time, though for a different purpose, and the village would indeed have seemed deserted then.

The Canadians suffered a higher casualty rate at Dieppe than they did in Normandy. Most of their tanks were destroyed before they could get off the beaches, and from this experience it is said many lessons were learned, including the need to develop 'floating' tanks for D-Day.

'Swimming' Sherman of 1st Cdn Hussars, now displayed in Normandy. The 'skirt' on the hull supported a canvas screen to achieve buoyancy.

Lord Mountbatten, then Chief of Combined Operations, said after the war: "The Battle of Normandy was won on the beaches of Dieppe. For every one man killed in Dieppe, at least ten more had their lives spared on the beaches of Normandy." Nonetheless, the Dieppe raid remains one of the most tragic and contentious events of the Second World War.

As a postscript, on 1st September 1944, during the rush to the Seine and Belgium following the defeat of the German Seventh Army in the 'Falaise Pocket', the 2nd Canadian Infantry Division captured Dieppe without a fight. This division consisted of the same brigades and the same regiments that had suffered on the raid two years previously, with one notable exception – the Calgary Regiment was then fighting in Italy.

To 'Juno Beach' and Beyond

In December 1942, a decision was made to reorganize the Canadian armoured regiments in preparation for specific roles in Normandy and elsewhere. The immediate effect of this, as far as the village was concerned, was to bring the Garrys back for their second visit to Headley (and the 1st Hussars back to Elstead). They were now destined to play an infantry support role in the D-Day landings on 'Juno' beach, forming the 3rd Canadian Tank Brigade (subsequently re-named 2nd Canadian Armoured Brigade) along with the Sherbrooke Fusiliers.

Meanwhile, units of the 4th Canadian Armoured Division had already passed through. Four regiments of this Division, the Governor General's Foot Guards, the Canadian Grenadier Guards, the British Columbia Regiment, and the South Alberta Regiment were destined to land in Normandy about a month after D-Day, to join up with and reinforce the 2nd Canadian Armoured Brigade forming the 2nd Canadian Corps and eventually the 1st Canadian Army. From then on they battled virtually side by side through France, Belgium and Holland to Germany. The Elgin Regiment was responsible for delivery of armoured vehicles to the combat zone.

It should be mentioned here that John Boxall, a long time resident of Headley after the war, also landed at Juno Beach on D-Day. He was in the RASC and part of a DUKW unit, bringing in troops and supplies in these amphibious vehicles. His widow Barbara tells us they had a live duck as their mascot which they took to Normandy with them. Just after the Canadians had landed, she says, the duck disappeared in mysterious circumstances, and nearly started World War III among the Allies. *So come on you Canadian guys – you can safely admit it now – who did for the RASC's duck?*

The 'Northern Ireland' Campaign

The Straths, previously colleagues and friendly rivals of the Garrys, and with them in Headley earlier in 1942, got what they considered at the time to be the better treatment – retained in the 5th Canadian Armoured Division as the *5th Canadian Armoured Brigade* along with the British Columbia Dragoons. On 12th November 1943 they boarded the "Scythia" at Avonmouth, thinking they were going to Northern Ireland – and arrived in Algiers at the start of the Italian campaign!

The Calgary Regiment, severely depleted after Dieppe, was 'reinforced, reorganized and retrained'. Their *Short History* records that they were given Rams in place of Churchills in November 1942 (presumably these were replaced by Shermans later) and in June 1943 the regiment embarked from Greenock for Sicily. There they distinguished themselves, fighting their way up through Italy as part of the *1st Canadian Armoured Brigade*. At the end of the Italian campaign they moved to NW Europe until the end of the war.

Juno Beach and Beyond

On the 50th anniversary of D-Day, I was privileged to introduce Canadian veteran Pat Lewis to a class of 14-year olds at a local school. They asked him some direct questions, and he gave them direct answers. Though the verse is mine, these are largely his words.

Fresh-faced fourteen, beautiful children,
boisterous scholars, with freedom to talk and argue,
make their point,
and put their hats on back to front, in England, 1994.

That's why we fought and many big men cried
on Juno Beach and through the weeks beyond.

"And did you hate the Germans?" –
Fifty years ago, we had a job to do,
a Bully, if you like, to put in place,
and men like us but dressed in grey had their job too.

We didn't know of Belsen, Auschwitz and the rest;
not then. Perhaps, who knows, if we'd known half the truth
we farmers from the prairies, loggers from the seaboard,
might have hated more the conscripts from the hamlets of the fatherland
who traded shots with us among the stinking orchards there in Normandy.
But as it was, we had a job to do,
a worth-while job, and did it to our best.

"How old were you?" –
Eighteen, and scared of never seeing nineteen,
never having all the good things life had promised,
scared of dying, but, above all, scared of showing I was scared.
Just eighteen,
volunteered at sixteen, anxious then to see the world,
and found my future led across the bar
of Juno Beach.

Eighteen,
but we were men compared with some of those in grey –
young boys, by-products of a system:
fresh-faced fourteen, beautiful children,
earnest students, with no freedom to talk or argue,
make their point,
or put their hats on back to front like you in England now.

So let me look at you again,
your cheeky grins, your mischievous ways;
and let me remember the reason why -
it was all for you, and your smiling eyes
that we soldiered on and comrades died
on Juno Beach and beyond.

John Owen Smith

After the War

It is perhaps some measure of the popularity of the Canadian troops in Britain that, at the end of hostilities, there were over 40,000 brides and 20,000 children waiting to be shipped to Canada to meet up with their Canadian husbands and fathers. Pete Friesen of the Garrys stayed on to help with the Canadian Wives' Bureau in London where they took 800 girls at a time into the Portman Hotel (there were also two other hotels) for one night before sending them by boat train to Southampton.

Pete himself married Enid, an English girl; his younger brother Dave married Betty, a Scottish girl; and his elder brother Jack ('Shorty') married Joan, a Welsh girl.

In Headley the redundant army huts were quickly occupied, legally or illegally, by those who would otherwise have been homeless. Tom Grisdale recalls: "I came back after the war, and we lived with mother-in-law for a while up Liphook Road till we eventually got this Nissen hut in Rectory Field. They were moving in all these displaced Poles and Ukrainians – you came home out of the army and you couldn't get anything.

"There were about 10 or 12 huts down by the side of the field opposite Tonards[†] – we were No 2. It was the remnants of an army camp, and squatters moved in after the army moved out. Then the Council took them over and put in a kitchen sink and a range, and made it into 3 rooms, but they could only brick it up three-quarters of the way because it was that shape, and if you got a frost, when it used to thaw out it was ghastly. All you had was a window at each end made of that reinforced glass so you couldn't see out. They gave you a bath which you hung on the wall and put down in front of the range."

Then in the early 50s: "We were about the second family to move into Erie Camp, No 7. They bricked up these huts which were one big room – not up to the ceiling, half way – and at one end they divided in the middle so you got two bedrooms and one big room. There was still the old tin roof, and with the condensation we had to put umbrellas over the bed and the cot. The floors were concrete – and where they'd been breaking up wood for burning it was like dust, so we put roofing felt down.

[†] The Rectory Field, behind the *Holly Bush*

"The Council put in a little range in the middle of this room, and you had one cold water tap, that's all. The toilet was a little wooden place outside with an earth bucket which the Council used to come round at midnight to empty, slopping it all up against the door. It wasn't bad – you had a bathroom with hot water and all that. We were happy there."

Tom also remembers: "When you dug in your garden, you dug up knives, forks, spoons – they buried everything, and the story is they even buried army motorbikes." They may or may not have buried motorbikes in Erie Camp; from recent stories in the local press, they do seem to have buried jeeps on Thursley Common, and Don Heather, as a lad, remembers seeing them burying a whole tank in a crater on Ludshott Common.

Over the years the huts disappeared from the village or were reused, in some cases more than once. One, for example, was moved to a site opposite Alex Johnston's house in Headley Fields and used as the village's Catholic Church until 1965, when a more permanent building was erected there. It was then moved again, this time to Beech Hill Road, and used as the Scout Hut until it finally burnt down spectacularly in 1985.

The huts at Erie Camp were replaced by council houses in the 60s and 70s, and this estate, now called Heatherlands, was eventually completed in 1978. The only reminder of its link with the Canadians is the name given to one of the roads there – 'Maple Way'.

Still We Remember

We cannot close this book without mentioning just a few examples of the happy memories which the name Headley evokes in many parts of Canada.

A young man from Headley Down went to work in Newfoundland in the fifties and met many Canadians there. They asked him from where he came. "Oh just a very tiny village called Headley Down." "Really? We know it well! We were in Erie Camp and on Ludshott Common during the war!"

When Barry and Wendy Ford moved into Erie Estate they had one of the first telephones, needing it to run their business, and he suggested she should surprise her aunt in Canada by giving her a call. "In those days you had to go through the operator", said Wendy. "The man in Canada asked me which exchange I was calling from, and was amazed when I told him Headley Down, saying he'd been at Erie Camp during the war – then when I said I was actually ringing from Erie Camp, he could hardly believe his ears. 'Of all the calls I could have answered!', he exclaimed – and we spent a long time chatting about Headley before I was put through to my aunt." She adds:" It's a pity, but I forgot to ask him his name."

More recently, Katie Warner was visiting her sons in Canada: "I got off the plane in Toronto one afternoon and a man just outside the door said, 'cab, madam?' – I said, 'no thank you', but he said, 'where do you come from?' I said, 'England, Hampshire' – 'What part?' – and I started to explain, and he said, 'Do you know Superior Camp? Do you know Erie?' and he went all round the camps, around Longmoor, Bordon, the lot, Huron – all of them – he said, 'I was there for about 4 years during the war' – and when I mentioned this part of Headley he said, 'I know it'. And another man I met actually knew the Congregational Institute – 'I know the house you lived in' – we were living in *The Old Manse* at one time."

Mary Fawcett started writing to a Canadian pen friend during the war, and they still correspond 51 years later. Lieut. Jack Casey of the Sherbrooke Fusiliers gave her the address of his sister-in-law Joan, who was two years older than Mary, being 13 while Mary was 11 years old. Jack, a "very handsome man" according to Mary, had opened his own restaurant in London, Ontario, before joining up in 1941 and coming to

England with his regiment late in 1942. He was billeted in *Kenton House* during his time in Headley, and is mentioned in Lt. Col. Jackson's book on the *Sherbrooke Regiment* for his 'coolness and disregard for personal safety' having saved the lives of a party of troopers at a grenade-throwing practice in Wales when one of them dropped his grenade with the pin pulled out.

Jack Casey landed on Juno Beach during the D-Day invasion, and received a severe head injury there. He was brought back to Brookwood Hospital, but sadly died of his wounds. However, Mary kept up her correspondence with Joan – they met for the first time on Mary's 21st birthday, and have continued to see each other many times since then.

While Jack Casey was in *Kenton House* he used to walk up to *Windridge*[†] in Headley Hill Road for meals. At the end of the war, a 'V-Day' meal was held there for the No.1 CACRU (Canadian Armoured Corps Reinforcement Unit). We don't know whether all these regiments were in Headley during the war – but if so, then at least 21 Canadian armoured units came rather than just the 13 mentioned opposite.

Those whose badges are shown (left to right) on the menu, above that of the Corps, are:

S.A.R.	South Alberta Regiment *[29]*
31 Recce	15th Alberta Light Horse *[31]*
12 Man. Dragoons	12th Manitoba Dragoons *[18]*
17 D.Y.R.C.H.	17th Duke of York's Royal Cdn Hussars *[7]*
4 P.L.D.G.	4th Princess Louise's Dragoon Guards *[4]*
R.C.D.	Royal Canadian Dragoons *[1]*
R.M.R.	Royal Montreal Regiment *[32]*
30 Recce	Essex Tank Regiment *[30]*
8 Recce	14th Canadian Hussars *[8]*
G.G.H.G.	Governor General's Horse Guards *[3]*

Note – Canadian Armoured Regiment Numbers shown thus: [32]

[†] See *I'Anson's Chalet on Headley Hill* by Judith Kinghorn for more information on *Windridge*.

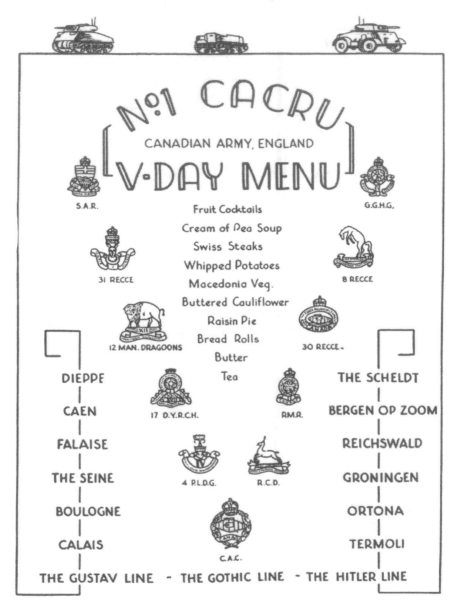

Nº1 CACRU
CANADIAN ARMY, ENGLAND
V·DAY MENU

S.A.R.

G.G.H.G.

Fruit Cocktails
Cream of Pea Soup
Swiss Steaks
Whipped Potatoes
Macedonia Veg.
Buttered Cauliflower
Raisin Pie
Bread Rolls
Butter
Tea

31 RECCE

8 RECCE

12 MAN. DRAGOONS

30 RECCE.

17 D.Y.R.C.H.

R.M.R.

4 P.L.D.G.

R.C.D.

C.A.C.

DIEPPE	THE SCHELDT
CAEN	BERGEN OP ZOOM
FALAISE	REICHSWALD
THE SEINE	GRONINGEN
BOULOGNE	ORTONA
CALAIS	TERMOLI

THE GUSTAV LINE – THE GOTHIC LINE – THE HITLER LINE

Appendix I

List of Canadian Regiments in the Headley Area

	Arr:	Dep:
Royal Provost Corps & RCMP [Erie Camp]		
Royal Canadian Army Service Corps		
Royal Canadian Engineers (various) [Erie]	May 41	???
Lorne Scots [Erie Camp]	Dec 41	Dec 41

1st Cdn Army Tank Bde + 3rd Cdn Inf Div

Calgary Regiment (14th C.A.R.) *HD*	Sep 41	Dec 41 to Seaford

Regina Rifles + possibly other infantry regiments with Calgary Regt?
 Also Ontario Regt. (11th C.A.R.) was somewhere in the vicinity.

5th Cdn Arm'd Div

Lord Strathcona's Horse (2nd C.A.R.) *HD*	Apr 42	Aug 42 to Hove
1st Hussars (6th C.A.R.) *EMT*	Apr 42	Aug 42 to Hove
Fort Garry Horse (10th C.A.R.) *L/H*	Apr 42	Aug 42 to Hove
British Columbia Dragoons (9th C.A.R.)	???	

4th Cdn Arm'd Div

Elgin Regiment (25th Recce Reg) *HD*	here with South Albertas	
South Alberta Regt (29th Recce Reg) *L/H* Aldershot	Sep 42	Jan 43 to
British Columbia Regt (28th C.A.R.) *EMT*	Sep 42	Feb 43 to Hove
Gov. Genl. Foot Guards (21st C.A.R.) *L/H*	Jan 43	Feb 43 to Hove
Cdn Grenadier Guards (22nd C.A.R.) *HD*		Feb 43 to Hove?

3rd Cdn Army Tank Bde (later re-named 2nd Cdn Arm'd Bde)

1st Hussars (6th C.A.R.) EMT	Feb 43	Jun 43 to Worthing
Fort Garry Horse (10th C.A.R.) *L/H*	Feb 43	Jun 43 to Worthing
Sherbrooke Fusiliers (27th C.A.R.) *HD*	Feb 43	Jun 43 to Worthing
16/22 Sask Horse (20th Recce Reg) *L/H*	Sum 43	Broken up: Nov 43
Essex Tank Regt (30th Recce Reg) *HD*	Aut 43	Broken up: Spr 44
Elgin Regiment (25th Recce Reg) *EMT*	Noted on 26 Nov 1943	

Notes:

C.A.R. =   Canadian Armoured Regiment.

Recce =   Armoured regiment equipped for reconnaissance.
 There were 31 Canadian Armoured and Recce regiments formed, of which 28 came to the UK. Nearly half of these appear to have visited the Headley area.

L/H = Lindford/Headley

HD = Headley Down

EMT = Elstead/Milford/Tilford. This location included here for completeness, since regiments of the same armoured Brigade or
 Division were stationed both here and at Headley, occasionally
 taking part in joint exercises.

Billet locations in the Headley area

Taking as an example the three regiments stationed simultaneously in our area in February 1943, the 3rd Canadian Army Tank Brigade (later renamed 2nd Canadian Armoured Brigade) is believed to have been billeted as follows:

1st Canadian Hussars – *Elstead/Milford/Tilford*

Regimental HQ & HQ Sqn	Elstead
A Squadron	Milford
B & C Squadrons	Tilford

Fort Garry Horse – *Lindford/Headley*

Regimental HQ & HQ Sqn	Lindford (Officers' mess Hilland)
A Squadron	Rectory Field
	(tanks Rogers Field; Officers' mess *Walden*)
B Squadron	Openfields (Officers' mess *Belmont*)
C Squadron	Barley Mow Hill & Hilland field
	(Officers' mess *Pound Cottage*)

Sherbrooke Fusiliers – *Headley Down*

Regimental HQ & HQ Sqn	The Mount
A Squadron	Ludshott Common
B Squadron	Beech Hill Rd/Headley Hill Rd
C Squadron	Crestafield
Intercommunication troop	Hearn

It is unclear whether other regiments distributed their squadrons in the same pattern.

D-Day at Juno Beach

The 2nd Canadian Armoured Brigade landed on D-Day at Juno Beach in support of the 3rd Canadian Infantry Division. Each of the three armoured regiments was assigned an infantry brigade, as shown in the diagram below:

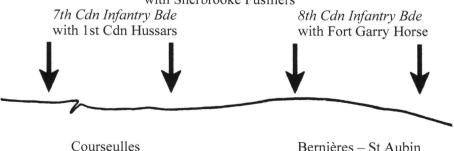

Naval Force 'J'

9th Cdn Infantry Bde
with Sherbrooke Fusiliers

7th Cdn Infantry Bde with 1st Cdn Hussars	*8th Cdn Infantry Bde* with Fort Garry Horse

Courseulles   Bernières – St Aubin

Appendix II

Calendar of events

1939
Sep 3   War declared by Britain on Germany
Sep 10   War declared by Canada on Germany
Sep 19   BEF lands in France.
Oct   South Staffordshire Regt arrives in Headley
Dec 7   'First flight' of Canadian troops embark – 7,400 men on 5 ships
1940
Mar   South Staffordshire Regt leaves Headley for BEF
May 10   Germans invade Belgium
May 20   Dunkirk evacuation of BEF
1941
Apr 12   Canadians take over responsibility from British Pioneer Corps
         for 'Camps being constructed from Canadian materials at
         Headley, Ludshott and Thursley'
May 6   Canadian camps in area formally named: Erie, Superior, etc
May 27   'D' Section of No.1 Road Construction Coy RCE at Erie Camp
Jul 1   Calgary Tank Regiment disembarks at Gourock
Aug 16   No.5 (then No.1) Cdn Construction Coy starts work on Erie
         Camp
Oct 2   Calgary Regiment arrives in Headley Down
mid Oct Engineers finish Erie Camp?
Oct 19   Trooper Nip Keys of Oshawa, Ont. signed his name in the
         Church Gate Stores attic
Oct 25   Automatic telephone exchange opened in Headley Down, on
         Glayshers Hill (opposite Erie Camp)
Nov 19   Calgary Regiment gets delivery of its first Churchill tanks (get
         full compliment only in May 1942)
Dec 2   Lorne Scots arrive to commission Erie Camp (leave 12 Dec)
Dec 18   Calgary Regiment leaves Headley Down for Seaford
1942
Apr 1   1st Cdn Hussars arrive in Elstead area
         Fort Garry Horse & Lord Strathcona's Horse arrive in Headley
         area
Apr 24   Review of 5th Cdn Armoured Div by King & Queen – Frensham
         Common
Jun 12   Garrys visited in Headley by Maj. Gen. Montague
Jun 15   James Desaulnier "came from Canada" – signature in Church
         Gate Stores
Jun 17   Lieut. Squires of the Straths killed falling from a tank in training
         on Ludshott Common
Aug 5/6 Fort Garry Horse & Ld Strathcona's Horse leave Headley, and
         1st Cdn Hussars leave Elstead area for Hove
Aug 8   Trooper Mitchell accidentally shot Trooper Brooks outside

	Church Gate Stores ('B' Squadron orderly room)
Aug 19	**Dieppe raid**: Calgary Regiment involved
Aug 20	T.R.P. J.L. Desaulnier F.G.H. D.R. signed his name again in the Church Gate Stores attic (see photo)
Sep 2/3	British Columbia Regiment arrives in Elstead area South Alberta Regt (& Elgin Regt?) arrive in Headley
Dec 17	Abnormal rains cause floods in Headley – report in *Herald*
Dec	Split up of Cdn Arm'd Divs: Straths, BC Dragoons and 8th Princess Louise NB Hussars stay with 5th Cdn Arm'd Div (destined for Italy); Garrys, 1st Hussars and Sherbrookes form new 2nd Arm'd (initially 3rd Army Tank) Brigade (destined for Normandy). "In the future the Canadian Armoured Divisions were to have only one brigade of tanks instead of two, following the precedent set by the enemy and afterwards by the British and Americans."

Elgin Regiment Squadron mascot 'Mr Chips', in Headley 1943

1943

Jan 13	Governor General's Foot Guards arrive in Headley
Jan 15	South Alberta Regt (& Elgin Regt?) leave Headley for Aldershot
Jan 28	Mayor Lewis of Ottawa visits Foot Guards in Headley
Feb 19	Foot Guards and Cdn Grenadier Guards leave Headley, and British Columbia Regiment leaves Elstead area for Hove
Feb 22	Sherbrooke Fusiliers & Garrys arrive in Headley 1st Cdn Hussars arrive in Elstead area
Mar 15	Tpr Michaelis killed Tpr Gibbs in a brawl near the Holly Bush
Apr 10	Garrys inspected in Bordon by Gen. Montague
Jun 1	Sherbrookes & Garrys leave Headley, and 1st Cdn Hussars leave Elstead area for Worthing
Jun 17	Calgary Regiment embarks for Sicily
Summ	16/22 Saskatchewan Horse arrive in Headley; later broken up
Fall	Essex Tank Regiment (30th Recce) comes to Headley – assembling trucks in Bordon
Nov 12	Straths embark for Algiers

1944

	RCEME run rehab course at Erie Camp
Mar 28	'Whitey', mascot of the Garrys, killed near Fawley
Spring	Essex Tank Regiment leaves Headley; later dispersed to other regiments
May	107 Regt (King's Own) RAC in Headley, waterproofing their Churchill tanks

William Curtis, Essex Tank Regt (30 Recce) taken in 1944

Jun 6	**D-Day**: Garrys, Sherbrookes and 1st Hussars land on Juno Beach
Jun 23	107 Regt (King's Own) RAC leaves Headley
Jul 1	107 Regt (King's Own) RAC lands on Juno Beach
July	4th Cdn Arm'd Div lands on Juno Beach
Oct 30	Princess Louise's Fusiliers arrive at Ludshott Common from Italy

1945

Jan 14	Frozen body of Pte Lasky of Princess Louise's Fusiliers found in water tank on Ludshott Common
May 8	Riot in Erie Camp on VE day
	V-Day Menu for No.1 CACRU

1948

July	Erie camp finally closed as a military establishment

1973

Sept	Last vestige of Erie Camp disappears when the last of the huts is demolished

Appendix III

Order of Battle for Canadian Regiments in 1945

<u>1st Infantry Division</u> *RED shoulder patches*
4th Princess Louise's Dragoon Guards (Recce) *[4]*
Saskatoon Light Infantry (M/c Gun Bn)
>**1st Infantry Brigade**
>Royal Canadian Regiment
>48th Highlanders of Canada
>Hastings & Prince Edward Regiment
>**2nd Infantry Brigade**
>Princess Patricia's Canadian Light Infantry
>Seaforth Highlanders of Canada
>Loyal Edmonton Regiment
>**3rd Infantry Brigade**
>Royal 22nd Regiment
>Carleton & York Regiment
>West Nova Scotia Regiment

<u>2nd Infantry Division</u> *ROYAL BLUE shoulder patches*
14th Canadian Hussars (Recce) *[8]*
Toronto Scottish (M/c Gun Bn)
>**4th Infantry Brigade**
>Royal Regiment of Canada
>Essex Scottish Regiment
>Royal Hamilton Light Infantry
>**5th Infantry Brigade**
>Black Watch of Canada
>Regiment de Maisonneuve
>Calgary Highlanders
>**6th Infantry Brigade**
>Fusiliers Mont Royal
>Queens Own Cameron Highlanders of Canada
>South Saskatchewan Regiment

<u>3rd Infantry Division</u> *FRENCH GREY shoulder patches*
17th Duke of York's Royal Canadian Hussars (Recce) *[7]*
Cameron Highlanders of Ottawa (M/c Gun Bn)
>**7th Infantry Brigade**
>Canadian Scottish Regiment
>Regina Rifles
>Royal Winnipeg Rifles
>**8th Infantry Brigade**
>Queens Own Rifles of Canada
>Regiment de la Chaudière
>North Shore Regiment
>**9th Infantry Brigade**
>Stormont Dundas & Glengarry Highlanders

North Nova Scotia Highlanders
Highland Light Infantry of Canada
4th Armoured Division *DARK GREEN shoulder patches*
South Alberta Regiment (Recce) *[29]*
    4th Armoured Brigade
    Governor General's Foot Guards *[21]*
    Canadian Grenadier Guards *[22]*
    British Columbia Regiment *[28]*
    Lake Superior Regiment (Motor Battalion)
    10th Infantry Brigade
    Argyll & Sutherland Highlanders of Canada
    Lincoln & Welland Regiment
    Algonquin Regiment
    New Brunswick Rangers (M/c Gun Bn)
5th Armoured Division *MAROON shoulder patches*
Governor General Horse Guards (Recce) *[3]*
    5th Armoured Brigade
    Lord Strathcona's Horse *[2]*
    8th Princess Louise's N.B. Hussars *[5]*
    British Columbia Dragoons *[9]*
    6th Duke of Connaught's R. Cdn Hussars (HQ Sqn) *[15]*
    Westminster Regiment (Motor Battalion)
    11th Infantry Brigade
    Irish Regiment of Canada
    Perth Regiment
    Cape Breton Highlanders
    Princess Louise's Fusiliers (M/c Gun Bn)
Independent Brigades *BLACK shoulder patches*
    1st Armoured Brigade
    Ontario Regiment *[11]*
    Three Rivers Regiment *[12]*
    Calgary Regiment *[14]*
    2nd Armoured Brigade
    1st Canadian Hussars *[6]*
    Fort Garry Horse *[10]*
    Sherbrooke Fusiliers *[27]*
Troops *ORANGE shoulder patches*
    1st Corps Troops
    Royal Canadian Dragoons (Recce) *[1]*
    2nd Corps Troops
    12th Manitoba Dragoons (Recce) *[18]*
    Prince Edward's Island Lt Horse (Corps HQ Defence) *[17]*
    Army Troops
    Elgin Regiment (Armoured Delivery) *[25]*
    Royal Montreal Regiment (HQ Defence) *[32]*

Note – Armoured Regiments numbered thus: [32]

Appendix IV

Specifications of Tanks

The following details *(except for notes in italics)* are copied from sheets of paper issued and notes taken in early 1943 by SG Vane-Hunt of *Square House*, Headley, at the Electrical and Mechanical Engineering School.

Survey of A.F.Vs in the Service – American Tanks

Note: ALL American tanks have the Engine and Clutch at the rear and the Transmission at the Front, with a Propeller Shaft in between. Tracks are built of rubber and steel. The rubber is vulcanised to the steel pivot pins.

Medium Tank M3 – General Grant I

Crew of Six: Commander, Driver, WT Op, 37 mm Gunner, 75 mm Gunner, Loader.

Weight 26 ton (30 US tons), length 17', width 8'11", height 9'11", ground clearance 24", fording depth 42", ground pressure 17.5 lb/sq in.

Armour plate thicknesses: front lower section 2", front upper section 1.5", sides & rear 1", ceiling & floor 0.5", turret cast armour 2", around pistol ports 3".

Armament:– Co-axial 37mm gun and .30 Browning in a power operated turret (combined electrical & hydraulic operation) and a 75mm gun in forward sponson.

Powered by a 400 BHP radial air cooled petrol engine at 2400 RPM. Engine has 9 cylinders and fan and flywheel are incorporated in one casting. Weight of engine and accessories 1,390 lbs – engine change in 7 hours with 'four good men'.

*(See notes on **Starting Procedure** following)*

Fuel capacity 150 galls.

Normal type clutch. Synchromesh gearbox (five forward and one reverse speed) with direct drive to a controlled differential.

Steering by application of brake bands to either side of the differential, so reducing the speed of one output shaft and proportionally increasing the speed of the other.

Drive from differentials to sprockets is through a double helical toothed reduction.

Suspension:– Three pairs of bogie wheels, each pair controlled by a volute spring.

British designed turret with no commander's cupola on top (unlike General Lee).

Medium Tank M3 – General Grant II

Similar to General Grant I, except that it is powered by twin 185 BHP GM two-stroke compression ignition engines at 2100 RPM.

A cross-drive carries the drive from the two engine clutches to the propeller shaft.

Both the 37mm and 75mm guns are fitted with gyro-stabilizers.

Medium Tank M4 – General Sherman

Weight 27 ton. Crew of five.

Armament:– Co-axial 75mm gun and .30 Browning in a power operated turret (combined electric and hydraulic operation). The gun is fitted with a gyro-stabilizer.

There are three types of hull used on this tank:–
1. Where all the hull is built up by riveting.
2. Where the top half of the hull is built up of welded plates.
3. Where the top half of the hull is a casting.

Experienced crews added old track links to the front armour of their Shermans for added protection.

The type of power unit will depend on the type of hull:–

Types 1 and 2 will be powered by either:
a). A twin 185 BHP GM two-stroke compression ignition engine at 2100 RPM, or
b). A Ford 8 cylinder V8 450 BHP petrol engine, or
c). A Chrysler 30 cylinder 500 BHP petrol engine using five engine blocks and crankshafts driving a single master pinion.

Type 3 will be powered by either:
a). A 400 BHP radial air-cooled petrol engine at 2400 RPM, of same design as the engine fitted to the General Lee, or
b). A nine cylinder Guiberson radial compression ignition engine of 400 BHP.

The transmission, steering, suspension and tracks are similar in design to the Generals Lee and Grant.

Note that Duplex Drive (DD) amphibious versions of the Sherman were produced which could swim ashore under their own power. They achieved buoyancy from a rubberized canvas screen attached to the hull deck. Two propellers were fitted to the rear of the tank, driven by off-takes from the rotating tracks, giving a speed through the water of approximately one hundred yards per minute. Steering was provided by a tiller. The screen doubled the tank's height and had to be collapsed quickly once ashore for the gun to be used. DDs were used with mixed fortunes on D-Day; some sank on their way to shore, but those that arrived proved very effective. There is an example on display in the Tank Museum at Bovington Camp, Dorset.

Medium Tank – Ram I

Canadian manufactured tank similar to the American Medium tank but equipped with a 2 Pdr.

Medium Tank – Ram II

Similar to the Ram I, but equipped with a 6 Pdr.

Ram tanks were retained for a number of operational roles: to be used as self-propelled guns; as flame throwers; or as 'kangaroo' troop carriers which, with turrets off, could transport infantry to the front at high speed.

General Grant – Starting Procedure

1. Make sure that the master switch and ignition switch are 'off' and that the gear lever is in neutral.
2. Check the level of the engine oil by the dipstick on the filter cap of the oil tank (do not overfill).
3. Inspect the engine compartment for loose and missing parts.
4. If engine has been stationery for five hours or more it must be turned by the starting handle over at least eight compressions (to check for a Hydrostatic Lock). If a lock is evident, remove spark plugs from lower cylinders to pump oil out.
5. Check the transmission and final driver for oil.
6. Check the voltmeter: it should read zero.
7. Close the master switch and the voltmeter should read 24 volts.
8. Turn on the required petrol tanks.
9. Turn on HYCON pressure cock and check for leaks.
10. Prime engine if necessary (not more than four pumps).
11. Check clearance of the clutch pedal and then depress it.
12. Close starter and booster switches together.
13. Let the engine turn for a short while then switch the magnetos on to 'Both'.
    NOTE:– Do not prime engine whilst it is turning or switched on.
14. Check oil pressure gauge: should read between 60–80 lbs per sq. in. (If the oil fails to show within 45 seconds, switch off the engine).
15. Check the flow of the gearbox oil by the tap situated at radiator.
16. Check for leaks throughout the engine and transmission.
17. Check the running of the engine on each of the magnetos.
18. Let the engine warm up before moving the tank. (The minimum oil temperature should be 80 degrees to 100 degrees).
19. Do not attempt to move off until engine has warmed up for at least 10 minutes.
NOTE:– If engine fails to start, check fuel cut-off valve for poor seating or sticking. Over priming and under priming will cause engine to be stubborn in starting.

Pat Lewis's comment: *"Can you imagine doing all this in action?"*

Appendix V

Extracts from the War Diaries
of the Fort Garry Horse regiment while in Headley
[thanks to The Fort Garry Horse Museum and Archives]

Their first week in Lindford & Headley:—

Wednesday 1/4/42: Cold and bright – Rain in afternoon. The Regiment left Aldershot and marched the 12 miles to their new quarters, arriving at 1500 hrs. Arrangements for their reception had been completed by the Advance Party and they were settled in quick order.

Thursday 2/4/42: Warm and bright. The day was spent in cleaning up areas. Sqn. locations were plotted. Officers get plenty of exercise walking between Messes and Orderly Rooms. The Auxiliary Services were already functioning with a show for the men at Hatch House Barn. The show "In Name Only".

Friday 3/4/42: Warm and bright with heavy rain in evening. Sqns continue work cleaning up in Sqn areas. Several keen gardeners have already put in small lots with various seeds. A Concert Party at the Headley Village Hall was very well attended and was pronounced a great success. Trooper Naylor of 'C' Sqn sustained injuries when he fell from a top bunk and was taken to 24th Fld Amb.

Saturday 4/4/42: Fairly warm with some cloudy periods. The Commanding Officer inspected the Sqn Areas this morning. Although a big improvement has been shown further attention is needed to bring them up to 'Garry' standards. Trooper Jorgensen of 'C' Sqn returning to his lines across country mistook a river for a road and arrived home somewhat damp.

Sunday 5/4/42: Very bright and warm. Church Parade to churches at Headley (Prot.) and Bordon (Cath). The afternoon was spent by most members of the Unit in exploring the countryside.

Monday 6/4/42: Cloudy with some showers. Normal training resumed throughout the Sqns. Classes on Browning, 37 millimetre, M3 Tank and 2 pounder are being held. Dance was held in Headley Village Hall.

Tuesday 7/4/42: Cloudy with rainy periods. Troops are beginning to feel at home in their new location and general opinion appears to be that it is preferred to Aldershot. Normal training continues.

Selection of entries until 21st August:—

Friday 10/4/42: Cloudy but clearing in afternoon. Normal Sqn training. Advanced driving training (unditching vehicles, road repairs, etc) is being instructed. The Regimental Dance Band which has been practising assiduously recently played for a Dance at Headley Village Hall. Although there was a slight scarcity of partners the evening and the Band were both successes.

Wednesday 15/4/42: Bright and clear. Cool. Normal Sqn. training. Bicycling is fast becoming the hobby and means of transportation of a number of officers and other ranks.

Saturday 18/4/42: Bright and clear. Ground is drying and mud has disappeared. Afternoon allotted to Sports. Baseball and Softball is very promising. The local residents are very interested but find it hard to understand. An 'Alert' was sounded at 0215 hrs and Sqn guards turned out. 5 bombs were dropped at some distance away to the South-West.

Friday 24/4/42: Cloudy and windy. Cool in morning. Becoming warm in afternoon. Unit moved to Frensham Common at 0900 hrs. At 1500 hrs 'Stand To' was sounded by Garry Trumpeters on the arrival of Their Majesties the King and Queen. After the Royal Salute was given Their Majesties made a tour of the Brigade in the field. Their Majesties displayed keen interest in the many phases of Armoured Corps Training which were being carried out. After the Inspection the entire Brigade doubled over to the Circle around their Majesties car and three cheers were given led by Brigadier Rutherford. Then the Westminster Band played 'Rule Britannia' and as the Royal Visitors moved off Lt-Col. Gianelli of the L.S.H. *[Lord Strathcona's Horse regiment, who were posted in Headley Down at this time]* led the Brigade in cheering.

Sunday 10/5/42: Dull and cloudy. Heavy rain during afternoon and evening. Softball game against 'A' Sqn had to be called off on account of heavy rain. Church parade to Headley for Protestants and Bordon for R.Cs. Regiment was ordered to stand by as result of fire at Grayshott early Sunday morning.

Friday 15/5/42: Misty and cool, warming and clearing in afternoon. All afternoon parades cancelled for Regimental Field Day. A real Success. Garden plots put in by different men are beginning to produce fresh vegetables.

Sunday 24/5/42: Cool and cloudy with intermittent showers. Recent rains greatly helped countryside as earlier dry weather had retarded growth and caused many heath fires. Church Parades to Headley and Bordon.

Tuesday 26/5/42: Cold and almost continuous rain. Range practices on Conford A/Tk Ranges with Browning. 300 Coax M.G. are being held for all tank crews on a basis of 65 per Sqn and 15 from R.H.Q. Coax practice is fired single shot as 2pdr as practice for when Unit goes on 2pdr ranges in Wales to fire.

Friday 29/5/42: Cool but mostly bright. Regtl Dance Band played to well-attended Dance at Headley Village Hall. Normal Training.

Wednesday 3/6/42: Very warm and bright. The Q.M. Staff have worked very hard arranging the Marquees for the Demonstration of all equipment on charge to the Regiment. 3 Marquees have been set up as well as the complete assortment of vehicles on charge to the Regiment, including their equipment. The Ministry of Information full length film 'Next of Kin' was shown to all ranks and was very favourably received. The film made a great impression from the Security point of view.

Friday 12/6/42: Cloudy with intermittent heavy showers. The Hon. Col. of the Regt. Major Gen. P.J. Montague inspected the Regt. at 1500 hrs on Headley Green. Our escort met him at 1155 hrs and conveyed him to the R.O.R. where he was met by the Commanding Officers Lt. Col. R.E.A. Morton. The party arrived at R.H.Q. mess at 1315 hrs where the following officers were introduced:—

Major E.B. Evans, 2i/c Regt. – Major H.C. Blandshard, O.C. 'H.Q' Sqn. – Major G.M. Churchill, O.C. 'A' Sqn – Major W.W. Halpenny, O.C. 'C' Sqn. – Capt. H.J. Peacey, O.C. 'B' Sqn – Capt. J.M. Bowie, Adjutant. – Capt. C.W. Bailey Ass't Adjutant – Lieut. H.M. Sleigh. – Lieut H. MacEwing, Paymaster – Brigadier J. Rutherford, O.C. 1 C.A.B. – Major Turnbull, B.M., 1 C.A.B.

Major Gen Montague was accompanied by Capt. Laury Andraine, Photographer who took pictures of the days proceedings. At 1400 Hrs he was taken for a drive in 'Royal Betty' commanded by Capt. A.S. [Alex] Christian. Upon return he inspected the Regt. At approx. 1600 hrs a picture was taken of the General and the Colonel surrounded by the Officers perched on a couple of General Lees. At 1700 hrs the party left for C.M.H.Q. escorted by the Regt'l D.R.'s. The General expressed his pleasure at the turn out of the Regt and addressed all Ranks while on Parade. The march past, led by the Regt'l band took place, saluting base being in front of old tree opposite 'A' Sqn orderly Room.

Monday 15/6/42: Clear and fairly warm. Normal training. The Unit was notified of a number of parcels and cigarettes lost by enemy action in transit here. Pay parade in evening for all Sqns. *[James Desaulnier signed 'came from Canada' in the Church Gate Stores attic on this date]*

Wednesday 17/6/42: Warm and bright. Normal training. Permission has been granted for men to wear shirtsleeves on duty and to and from meals providing web belts are worn during the warm weather. *[Lieut. Squires of the Lord Strathcona's Horse regiment was killed falling from a tank in training on Ludshott Common this day — but not mentioned in the Garry's diary]*

Friday 19/6/42: Warm with some cloudy periods. Still a large number of men proceeding on various courses. The talk of the 'Second Front' is main topic among the men.

Wednesday 24/6/42: Still remaining dry and clear. Crops in locality need rain. Inter Sqn ball games etc in afternoon. Regt'l tennis Doubles tournament started.

Wednesday 1/7/42: *[Dominion Day]* Cloudy, rather cool in morning. Proclaimed a holiday although training continued on Ludshott Common and firing parties were on Conford Ranges.

Saturday 4/7/42: Cloudy, showers. Training carried out all day on Ludshott Common and Conford Ranges. D38025 Tpr. Fine J. 'H.Q.' Sqn, was tried by Court Martial and found guilty by the Court of striking a superior Officer. Court held in Hatch House Barn.

Wednesday 8/7/42: Bright and warm. Occasional Clouds. The Regt paraded at 'H.Q.' Sqn Vehicle Park at 1600 Hrs and then marched to Bordon station. *[Arrived Pembroke 0630 Hrs. next day. R.C.A.S.C. Vehicles convoyed the Unit to Merrion Camp. Gun firing practice at*

Linney Head over the next few days.]

Friday 17/7/42: Cloudy occasional showers. The Regt returned to Lindford and Headley leaving Pembroke in the Morning. Haversack lunch was carried and tea was obtained at Bristol. Regt'l Convoy from Bordon Station to Sqn Areas.

Saturday 18/7/42: Sky overcast, showers. Rear party returned from Merrion Camp. General settling down after return from Wales. Picture show Headley Village Hall in the evening.

Sunday 19/7/42: Bright not very warm. Church parades to Headley Church and Halehouse Chapel.

Sunday 26/7/42: Bright, warm. Church parade to Headley Church. After the Service a march past was held Lt Col Morton taking the salute. The saluting base was under the large tree opposite the Holly Bush Inn, Headley.

Wednesday 29/7/42: Bright, warm. Advance party packed and loaded ready to move to new location at Hove on the South Coast. Normal training for the Remainder of the Regt. Brigade Quiz on Map Reading, Field craft, Etc.

Saturday 1/8/42: Bright and warm. There was a Regtl Parade at St Lucia Barracks to-day — Lt Col R.E.A. Morton inspected the Regt and afterwards took the salute as the Regt marched past first in Column of Troops then in Column of Route. The officers held a garden party in the afternoon at Pound Cottage ('C' Sqn officers Mess) Headley. The was well attended by local inhabitants as well as a number of Officers and their Ladies from our own and other Units.

Thursday 6/8/42: Dull in the morning, clearing up in the afternoon. Reveille was early this morning also Breakfast. Kitchen vehicles and baggage was quickly loaded. Echelon Rdv at 'B' Sqn Tank party and proceeded to Frensham Common thence to Hove. There was one casualty enroute when an 'A' Sqn lorry turned over in the ditch. The driver suffered minor injuries.

Saturday 8/8/42: Dull with overcast sky. Some light showers in the late afternoon and evening. The Regt is pretty well settled down with only a few minor details to be seen to. Lt Col Morton spoke to all ranks this morning on the new phase of training that we are going into. An area on the South Downs Training area has been allotted to us. This evening there were several short Air Raid warnings. When the sirens went for the last warning immediately the A/A Guns opened up. This was the first time most of the men had heard A/A fire and there was plenty of excitement. It was reported that an enemy plane was shot down over the Channel. H26532 Tpr. Brooks R.A. was accidentally shot by B61419 Tpr. Mitchell W.E. at Headley where both men were on the Regt'l Rear Party *[Occurred outside the Church Gate Stores building]*.

Wednesday 12/8/42: Cloudy, light scattered showers. This afternoon H26532 Tpr. Brooks, R.A. was buried in Brookside Cemetery with full Military Honours. There was an alert this morning early and local A/A opened fire.

Friday 14/8/42: Bright and warm. Sqn Training. There was a short Alert early this morning also one at noon today. The regt was paid this evening. A court of enquiry was held today at Winchester, Hants. for the purpose of inquiring into the circumstances surrounding the death of H26532 Tpr. Brooks, R.A. President – Major E.B. Evans, Members – Capt. C.M. McLean, and Lieut. W.E.A. McMithell.

Wed 19/8/42: Bright and Warm, light showers in evening. Normal training for Sqns. Great excitement throughout the Regt on hearing the news of Canadian and Allied Landings at Dieppe. Continuous stream of British planes over here on route to French coast. This afternoon one of our ships was bombed just off shore and our shore batteries opened up. The plane was brought down. Bde orders in at 1640 hrs for men to pack and make ready to move. Bde conferences at 1700 hrs. However no counter measures were taken by the enemy, but the general feeling of being close to action has proved a marvellous boost to the morale and the keenness of the men.

Thursday 20/8/42: Bright and warm. Normal training. Some enemy activity overhead in the evening and local A/A batteries opened up. The Garry Volleyball team beat the Westminster and LSH teams to win the Brigade Championship. *[Trooper J.L. Desaulnier F.G.H. D.R. signed his name again in the Church Gate Stores attic in Headley]*

Friday 21/8/42: Bright and warm. Some scattered showers in evening. Normal training. Rear party returned from Headley. The Regimental Volleyball Team carried on their record by winning the Divisional Championship.

The regiment moved on to Crowborough in October, and back to Hove in December. On 11th January 1943, they heard with disappointment that they were to be reassigned to a new Brigade, and were moved back inland to Aldershot. Then on 22nd February 1943, they were posted to Lindford & Headley again ... where they were to remain until June of that year.

We pick up the Diary while the Regiment was still stationed in Hove, and received the news that the Canadian Army was to be reorganised. This was not greeted with great enthusiasm, and made for one of the longest entries of any day in the Diary:—

Monday 11/1/43: There was an Officers' meeting in the evening when the Colonel delivered a momentous address. There had been a reorganization of the Canadian Army, modelled along the British lines. There will be only one Armoured Bde in an Armoured Division. The result is that this unit, with the First Hussars, leaves the 5 Armd Div. and becomes part of the 3 Cdn Armd Bde, along with the Sherbrook Fusiliers of the 5 Div. Under Brigadier Bradbrooke.

Our present Brig – Brig J.T. Rutherford – takes command of the 11 Inf Bde in the 5 Div. The G.G.H.G. *[Governor General's Horse Guard]* become the Recce unit of the 5 Div. The R.C.D.s *[Royal Canadian Dragoons]* are Corps or Army Recce. The Officers mess is stunned by this news. Although they knew that the Cdn Army was to be

90

reorganized, the completeness of the change was not visualized by anyone.

Why the unit which is by far the best unit in the Div, as can be shown by results of Div and Bde Inspections, by Linney head, by Sports results, by results of Officers and O.R.s on courses, by our reputation in the Canadian Army generally, by our reputation with the civilians where ever we have been stationed, by the fact that our leadership is by far the most able in the Div, by the fact that our men are head and shoulders above the general caliber, by the fact that we have managed by the sheer weight of our ability to make the Brigadier who at first did not favour us, claim that we were the best unit in his Bde and by the thousand other factors, why this unit was left paraded to Lieut. Gen. A.G.L. McNaughton on our behalf, our honorary Colonel Major Gen Montague did likewise and our Colonel went to see Gen McNaughton but Gen Montague saw him on his behalf. Gen. McNaughton's attitude was that this was not a kick in the pants but merely a change, that our new Bde under Brig Thomas formerly of the 3 Armd Bde (now deceased) was likely to see action as soon as the 5 Armd Bde.

The feeling in the unit is that although it is a blow to our pride, we can turn it into our favour. We realize that geographical considerations (one unit from the East, one from the West and one from the Pacific) had to be considered in the changing of the set-up of the Canadian Army. The Ld. S.H. stayed in the 5 Div because they were an excellent unit P.F. But there is also a feeling that questions of Political expediency may have been considered. We hope not—we hate to think that others have received favours out of line with their merits. So we take things on their face value and say that the 3 Cdn Army Tank Bde is just as important as the 5 Cdn Armd Bde. Besides, if it is not, the Fort Garry Horse and the First Hussars (past slight differences forgotten) will make it so. Our leadership is too good and ability too definite to be permanently set back by blows to our pride.

We still have our Rams *[a Canadian-built version of the Sherman]* which is a great help. For all and sundry we issue the warning that there were no better Armoured units than ourselves and there will be no better Army Tank Units and that includes the first Army Tank Bde (of which we were once a part, for about a month).

The attitude of the unit is that we have the ability and that we will display it on the field of battle as did our unit in the last war. We were the only Militia unit in the Canadian Army in the last war to keep its entity and that entity cannot be lost.

But the most interesting result of the reorganisation from our point of view was that the Regiment found itself posted back to Headley again:—

Monday 22/2/43: The Regiment moved off at 1000 hrs (from Aldershot) and arrived in the Lindford and Headley areas at 1130 hrs. The run was well handled and no accidents occurred. The remainder of the day was spent in doing maintenance and getting settled in the barracks. Offices were set up.

Tuesday 23/2/43: Tpr. Lalonde A.J., who won the British Empire Medal last November, and two of his friends, namely, Tpr Conway V.G.H. and Tpr Fidler C. left for Buckingham Palace this morning to attend an Investiture held there by the King. His Majesty shook hands with Tpr Lalonde and pinned a Medal on his chest.

Wednesday 24/2/43: A show called 'Escape to Glory' was put on in Hatch House barn by the Salvation Army.

Sunday 28/2/43: There were Church parades to Headley Parish Church for the Protestants and to Headley Village Hall for the R.C.s. The afternoon as usual was free.

Monday 1/3/43: Lieut. H.E. [Harvey] Theobald took over the post of Regimental Intelligence officer today. Lieut R.D. [Bob] Grant was posted to the newly formed Recce troop.

Wednesday 3/3/43: In the afternoon there was a football game between our unit team and the Sherbrook Fusiliers. Our unit won three to nothing. This evening there was a show (Shall We Dance) put on in the Hatch House Barn by the Salvation Army.

Thursday 4/3/43: Four German airmen escaped in a Canadian Staff car from Crawley Sussex today. At 1600 hrs Capt D.S. [Buck] Whiteford of 'C' Squadron saw a staff car which was thought to be the stolen car.

Friday 5/3/43: In the afternoon there was a Soccer playoff game at Daly Field in Bordon between our unit team and the South Alberta Regiment. The South Alberta Regiment won by a margin of 8-4.

Sunday 7/3/43: There was an R.C. Church parade this morning to Grayshott where Brigadier A.M. Thomas attended with his staff. After Church there was a march past of all Brigade R.C.s with Brigadier Thomas taking the salute. An English Armoured Corps Band played for this parade. The Protestants Church parade was to Headley Parish Church where they saw the graves of Canadian soldiers who died in the last war [Bramshott?–Ed]. During the night there was an air raid during which some new Anti-personnel bombs were dropped. Incendiary bombs caused heath fires on the London – Liphook road. There was also a high explosive bomb dropped near the Hindhead Hospital.

Wednesday 10/3/43: There was a Mobile Bath at HQ Squadron today. This evening there was a dance in Headley Hall.

Thursday 11/3/43: This evening there was a picture show (Sergeant York) shown in the N.A.A.F.I. on Headley Green.

Monday 15/3/43: [Tpr Michaelis brawled with Tpr Gibbs near the *Holly Bush* – see 26 March]

Tuesday 16/3/43: Clear and cold becoming warmer on the day. On this morning's parade there were new mugs issued to the men. Normal training was carried out for the remainder of the day.

Friday 26/3/43: Corporal J.T. Gibbs died today from injuries received on March 15.

Saturday 27/3/43: At 1430 hrs today Lieut H.E. [Harvey] Theobald and Delores Irene Pidgin of Headley were united in marriage at St Joseph's

Church at Grayshott. Immediately after the reception they left on their honeymoon. There was a range run this afternoon in which a number of competitors from each Squadron ran to Conford Ranges and then fired five application shots.

Monday 29/3/43: The Squadron O.C.'s and 2 i/c's plus the Intelligence staff proceeded to Hankley Common this morning to watch a demonstration on the handling of prisoners of war upon capture.

Tuesday 30/3/43: There were pay parades form 1230 hrs to 1800 hrs being paid in the following order 'A' 'B' 'C' and 'HQ'. On these parades all men and N.C.O.'s turned out in light battle order and carried rubber boots.

Wednesday 31/3/43: This afternoon there was a group of personnel from each Squadron attended Corporal Gibbs's funeral

Sunday 4/4/43: The Regt advanced their time one hour.

Saturday 10/4/43: The Regiment went to 'Martinique' parade square in 'Camp Bordon' and practised Squadron and Regimental drill. There were marches past, first in line then in column. This was for an inspection by Major General The Hon. P.J. Montague our Hon. Col. After dismissal there was a Regimental 'Victory Week' party. There were also races, rides in peeps and carriers and other entertainment for the children. The proceeds were 27 pounds.

Sunday 11/4/43: There was a R.C.'s Church parade to Headley Village Hall at 0900 hrs this morning. The Protestants turned out S.A.P. at 0945 hrs dressed in best battle dress, web belts, black gloves and berets. They were transported to 'Grayshott' where they dismounted and marched to 'St Albans' Church in 'Hindhead'. On the way to the Church there was a march past with Brigadier A.M. Thomas taking the salute. The party arrived back in camp at 1250 hrs.

Tuesday 13/4/43: This evening from 2100 hrs until 2200 hrs there was a steady stream of heavy bombers passing over head proceeding due South.

Friday 23/4/43: This evening there was an air raid alert about 2230 hrs. Explosions were heard in the distance and aircraft motors were heard over head, but there was no local A.A. fire.

Tuesday 4/5/43: The usual Tuesday morning Respirator period was held this morning. 'A' Sqn went through the Gas Chamber and the Dental Clinic today. 'C' Sqn was at Thursley Common training with #1 C.L.R.U. 'B' Sqn carried out normal training all day.

Friday 7/5/43: There was a practice harbour scheme today in preparation for the coming Bde Scheme. Tanks were stowed in the afternoon and kits packed for the scheme tomorrow. Some of our Tank crews returned with some new tanks which were equipped with steel tracks and the new Stabilizers. The Regt left this evening on the Bde scheme.

Saturday 8/5/43: Broke harbour in the morning and proceeded to Basingstoke where another harbour was set up at noon. They remained there all day and slept there that night.

Sunday 9/5/43: Broke camp at 0300 hrs at Basingstoke and proceeded eastward where they set up a crash harbour four miles North of Farnborough at approx noon. Arrived back at camp at 1500 hrs.

Monday 10/5/43: Capt A.S. [Alex] Christian gave a lecture on his experience in North Africa with the first army.

Wednesday 12/5/43: In the evening all of the Officers and some of the N.C.O.s attended a lecture at the Sally Lund Café on 'What to do if you become a prisoner of War'.

Friday 14/5/43: Twenty all Ranks were invited to a dance arranged by the Women's Land Army.

Saturday 15/5/43: Part of the Regt this morning for Salisbury Plains to take part in a practice demonstration for the War Office. An ENSA concert was held in the Headley Village Hall.

Monday 17/5/43: The Regt with the exception of those at Salisbury Plains proceeded to Hankley Common today to practice for the coming inspection of the Bde by a distinguished dignitary of England.

Tuesday 18/5/43: Two more tanks were delivered to the Regt today bringing our total number up to fifty. This is the largest number that the Regt has ever had at its disposal at one time.

Wednesday 19/5/43: This morning His Royal Highness the Duke of Gloucester inspected the Bde at Hankley Common. First His Highness watched a tank demonstration by Bde tank crews and then he drove slowly through the lines of men of the Bde who were a file along both sides of the road. As he approached each Regt he was greeted with three rousing cheers. *[The Sherbrooke Fusiliers note that they extinguished fires on Ludshott Common this afternoon, started by their own mortars!]*

Monday 24/5/43: The Regt was issued orders to move to the Worthing area by June the first. The advance party left this morning.

Wednesday 26/5/43: Most of the day was spent in packing and preparation for the coming move. Maintenance and stowing was done on the tanks and other tracked vehicles.

Thursday 27/5/43: The tanks were loaded on transporters so as to be ready to move off early in the morning.

Monday 21/5/43: Final clean up and inspection and inspection and loading of equipment took place today. Tonight the personnel had to sleep outside so that things would be cleaned up and ready for an early start in the morning.

Tuesday 1/6/43: Bright and fairly warm with a few passing clouds. Reveille at 0400 hrs cleaning up of sleeping areas commenced immediately. All personnel were in 'A' Sqn Vehicle Park by 0545 hrs ready to move off. The move began at 0545 hrs and the convoy arrived in Worthing at 0930 hrs.

So the Fort Garry Horse Regiment finally bade farewell to Headley. They were to embark for 'Juno Beach' a year later in support of the 8th Canadian Infantry Brigade as part of the D-Day landings.

Appendix VI
List of Contributors & Acknowledgements

From the Village:

Sue Allden	Don Heather
Grace Barnes	Elsie Johnson
Barbara Boxall	Dot Myers
Jim Clark	Fred & Betty Parker
Arthur Dean	Betty Roquette
Joyce Dickie	Joyce Stevens
John Ellis	David Sulman
David & Mary Fawcett	Paula Wadhams
Wendy Ford	Katie Warner
Tom & Barbara Grisdale	David Whittle

and the many others who have given their help, advice and information so willingly.

From the Regiments:

Patrick Lewis	(Sherbrooke Fusiliers)
E C (Ted) Brumwell	(Fort Garry Horse)
Pete Friesen	(Fort Garry Horse)
Bob Grant	(Fort Garry Horse)
Erle Kitching	(Fort Garry Horse)
Harvey Theobald	(Fort Garry Horse)
Rod Waples	(Fort Garry Horse)
Tom Webb	(Fort Garry Horse)
Charles Wendover	(Fort Garry Horse)
John Whitton	(Fort Garry Horse & Calgary)
Harvey Williamson	(Fort Garry Horse)
William Curtis	(Essex Tank Regiment)
Marcel Fortier	(Governor General's Foot Guards)
Al Trotter	(16/22 Saskatchewan Horse)
Dennis Scott	(Calgary)
Len Ford	(RCE)
Phil Herring	(RCE)
Fergus Steele	(RCE)
Anthony John Vella	(RCE)
Stan Williams	(RCE)
Len Carter	(1st Canadian Parachute Battalion)
'Slim' Bradford	(various)

Other Acknowledgements:

Glenn Wright, Staff Historian, RCMP Ottawa
Access to History Publications, Ottawa – for *Battle-dress Patrol*
Staff of *Legion* Magazine, Ottawa
Vic Waller – information about Canadian forces Order of Battle
Staff of Aldershot Military Museum
Staff of Imperial War Museum, London
Staff of The Tank Museum, Bovington Camp
Roger & Lyn Butcher – *Church Gate Stores*
Jane Durham – information about Ludshott Common
Pauline Grove – letters of Herbert Price
Vivien Hardy – information about British D-Day landings
Mr & Mrs Bill Hinson – *Headley Mount Cottage*
Carl Tantum – information about Headley Catholic Church
Gord Crossley – Fort Garry Horse Museum
Ralph Howlin – photos sent to *Holly Bush* pub
Widow of Alex 'Danny' Getz – photograph

References:

Vanguard – the Fort Garry Horse in the Second World War,
   by Col. R E A Morton
Lord Strathcona's Horse in the Second World War,
   by Lt. Col. J M McAvity
The Sherbrooke Regiment, by Lt. Col. H M Jackson
A Short History of the 29 Cdn Arm'd Recce Regiment,
   by Maj. G L Macdougall
The Calgary Regiment – a short history
A History of the First Hussars Regiment 1856–1945
Battle-dress Patrol, the military contribution of the RCMP to the Canadian
   Provost Corps 1939–45, by Commissioner L H Nicholson
1st Battalion The Regina Rifle Regiment 1939–1944
The Story of the British Columbia Regiment 1939–1945
Light Dragoons, by Allen Mallinson
The Half Million, by C P Stacey & Barbara M Wilson
British and Commonwealth Armoured Formations 1919–46
   by Duncan Crow
Dieppe 1942, by Ronald Atkin
The Churchill, by Bryan Perrett
Wartime copies of *The Herald*

Other books of local interest:—

Headley's Past in Pictures—a tour of the parish in old photographs
Headley as it was in the first half of the 20th century. In this book you are taken on an illustrated tour of the parish by means of three journeys.
ISBN 978-1-873855-27-0 December 1999, updated 2003, over 100 photographs, plus historical notes and maps of the area.

I'Anson's Chalet on Headley Hill—a hidden house, a hidden history
Hidden among the pine trees on Headley Hill there is a Swiss-style chalet. Who built it and why? Judith Kinghorn investigates the history of her house *Windridge* and discovers a fascinating cast of characters.
ISBN 978-1-873855-48-5 October 2004, illustrated.

Walks Around Headley ... and over the Borders
A dozen circular walks starting from Headley.
ISBN 978-1-873855-49-2 May 2005, notes, illustrations and maps.

Walks Through History – at the West of the Weald
A dozen local walks with a historical theme by John Owen Smith.
ISBN 978-1-873855-51-5 December 2006, notes, illustrations and maps.

To the Ar and Back—an historical stroll around Headley and Arford
Joyce Stevens tells us the history of forty-seven locations within a mile of the centre of Headley. Illustrated with line drawings by Mick Borra.
The Headley Society, 1992, updated 2003 illustrations plus map.

The Southern Wey—a guide, by The River Wey Trust
Details of the Southern River Wey from its source near Haslemere through Headley parish to Tilford where it joins the northern branch.
ISBN 978-0-9514187-0-3 reprinted January 1990, well illustrated.

One Monday in November ... and beyond
The full story of the Selborne & Headley workhouse riots of 1830.
ISBN 978-1-873855-33-1 Republished September 2002, illustrations & maps.

Heatherley – by Flora Thompson – *her sequel to the 'Lark Rise' trilogy*
The book which Flora Thompson wrote about her time in Grayshott – the 'missing' fourth part of her *Lark Rise to Candleford* collection.
ISBN 978-1-873855-29-4 September 1998, notes, illustrations and maps.

On the Trail of Flora Thompson – from Grayshott to Griggs Green
Discovering the true life of Flora Thompson as she describes it in *Heatherley*.
ISBN 978-1-873855-24-9 First published May 1997, updated 2005.

Other books of local interest (continued):—

Ancient Churches in North East Hampshire – Twelve fascinating churches in the north east corner of Hampshire. A map on the back cover guides you through the picturesque lanes of the area, and 33 photographs give both exterior and interior views of each church. As well as Headley, the book includes Alton, Bentley, Binsted, Bramshott, Froyle, Hartley Mauditt, Holybourne, Kingsley, Selborne, and East & West Worldham. A short glossary is included for those unfamiliar with some of the architectural terms used. Suitable size for the pocket.
ISBN 978-1-873855-11-9 April 1995, illustrations plus map.

A Parcel of Gold for Edith– letters from the Australian goldfields to England 1853–1875 by Joyce Stevens
The story of one of Australia's Pioneer Women who in 1841, aged only 19, fled poverty in Portsmouth and set off alone to live in the new colony of Victoria. Her story has been pieced together by her gt-gt-granddaughter from the discovery of seven letters written to her brother, William Suter, a papermaker in Headley.
ISBN 978-1-873855-36-2 November 2001, illustrated plus maps.

Grayshott – the story of a Hampshire village by J. H. (Jack) Smith
The history of Grayshott from its earliest beginnings.
ISBN 978-1-873855-38-6 First published 1976, republished 2002, illustrated.

Churt: a Medieval Landscape by Philip Brooks
A remarkable insight into the world of ox plough teams, hand-sown crops and a community whose very survival was dependent on the produce of the land. *ISBN 978-1-873855-52-2 First published 2000, republished 2006, illustrated.*

Shottermill – its Farms, Families and Mills by Greta Turner
A history of Shottermill and the area around – where the counties of Hampshire, Surrey and Sussex meet. *Two volumes.*
ISBNs 978-1-873855-39-3 & 978-1-873855-40-9 Published 2004/2005.

The Hilltop Writers—a Victorian Colony among the Surrey Hills, by W.R. (Bob) Trotter
Rich in detail yet thoroughly readable, this book tells of sixty-six writers including Tennyson, Conan Doyle and Bernard Shaw who chose to work among the hills around Haslemere and Hindhead in the last decades of the 19th century.
ISBN 978-1-873855-31-7 Illustrated version, published March 2003.

John Owen Smith, publisher — www.johnowensmith.co.uk